SUCCINCT AND SELECT

THEOLOGICAL APHORISMS

IN TWENTY-THREE CHAPTERS
CONTAINING THE CORE OF ALL THEOLOGY
DRAFTED AND ADAPTED FOR USE IN
SCHOLASTIC DISPUTATIONS

by Johann Gerhard
Doctor of Theology and Superintendent at Heldburg

With the grace and privilege of the Elector and the Dukes of
Saxony
Jena

published by
Tobias Steinmann
1611

translated by Paul A. Rydecki

Repristination Press
Malone, Texas

Succinct and Select Theological Aphorisms... is translated from the original Latin work entitled Original title: *Aphorismi Succincti et Selecti, in Viginti Tribus Capitibus, totius Theologiae nucleum continentes (1611)*. Copyright 2018 by Paul A. Rydecki. Published by permission of the translator. No part of this publication may be reproduced, stored in a retrieval system, or transmitted in any form or by any means, electronic, mechanical, photocopying or otherwise without the prior written permission of Repristination Press.

Published in 2018

REPRISTINATION PRESS
716 HCR 3424 E
MALONE, TEXAS 76660

www.repristinationpress.com

ISBN 1-891469-76-2

Table of Contents

Dedicatory Letter		5
Chapter 1	Sketch of Theological Headings	13
Chapter 2	The Holy Scripture	19
Chapter 3	God	27
Chapter 4	The Person and Office of Christ	35
Chapter 5	Creation and the Angels	45
Chapter 6	Providence	51
Chapter 7	Election and Reprobation	57
Chapter 8	The Image of God in Man after the Fall	63
Chapter 9	Original Sin	71
Chapter 10	Free Will	79
Chapter 11	The Law	85
Chapter 12	The Gospel	91
Chapter 13	Repentance	101
Chapter 14	The Faith by Which We Are Justified before God	111
Chapter 15	Good Works	121
Chapter 16	The Sacraments	131
Chapter 17	Holy Baptism	141
Chapter 18	The Holy Supper	153
Chapter 19	The Church	165
Chapter 20	The Ecclesiastical Ministry	173
Chapter 21	The Political Order	183
Chapter 22	Marriage	191
Chapter 23	The Four Final Things that Await Man	197

Dedicatory Letter

To a courageous and capable man, most noble in splendor of birth, erudition, authority, and virtues, my most honorable patron and sponsor, Lord Balthasar of Wangenheim, hereditary elder in greater Behringen, etc.:

O courageous and capable man, most noble in every way, most honorable patron and sponsor, no one doubts that in order rightly to attend to the areas of the Church's ministry, among other things, it is especially required that the bishop be able not only to encourage in sound doctrine, but also to convict those who contradict, as the apostle teaches in Titus 1:9. Just as those working to repair the city and temple of Jerusalem stood with their swords girded, at the order of Nehemiah, carrying out the labor with one hand and holding a shield in the other (Neh. 4:17), so also the ministers of the Church who labor to build the spiritual house of God, as those standing on a perpetual line of battle, must not only edify with sound doctrine, but also drive away the enemies of the heavenly truth with the sword of the Spirit.

Just as it is the duty of a good shepherd not only to lead the sheep entrusted to his care to green pastures, but also to defend them along the way from the insidious attacks of the wolves, so it is necessary for those shepherds and bishops whom the Holy Spirit has placed over the Lord's flock not only to shepherd the Church of God (Acts 20:28), but also bravely to drive away false prophets—those ravenous wolves (Mat. 7:15)—from the sheepfold of the Lord. As a twofold purpose is set before a doctor, namely, to preserve present health and to restore the health that has been damaged (Galen's *1. de sanit. Tuenda*, cap. 1. and elsewhere, *Concil. diff.*

3. *Celsus* lib. 5. cap. 26.), for which reason two main areas of medicine are established, hygienic and therapeutic, so also in the case of those to whom the spiritual care of souls has been committed, it is beneficial not only to inform the hearers entrusted to their care with the true and sound doctrine, but also to preserve them with all diligence from the heresies which are like a plague, like gangrene (2 Tim. 2:17).

Therefore, says Augustine (4. *de doctr. Christ.* cap. 4.), the minister "should be a handler and a teacher of the divine Scriptures, a defender of the true faith and a vanquisher of error. He should both teach the good and unteach the bad. And in this work of preaching, he should win over the hostile, rouse the remiss, inform those who do not know what to do or what they should expect." To be sure, it is especially to this end that those scholastic exercises called 'disputations' have been instituted, which, aside from their other benefits—and these are very great indeed—form the minds of students beyond their studies, so that they are able to oppose the adversaries of the heavenly doctrine and convince them by the power of the Spirit. Disputations are what free youthful minds from the disease of self-love and from the vain conceit of wisdom. Disputations are what confirm, in no small way, the full assurance of faith in the heart. Disputations are what show us the way, as a lamp, to illuminate the more obscure passages of Scripture, to win over those who appear to contradict themselves, and to provide the correct answers to difficult questions. It is clear just how valuable and how customary they have been, from the earliest times of the ancient Church. They were initiated and consecrated by Christ, who, at the age of twelve, sat in the Temple in the midst of the teachers and listened to them and questioned them (Luke 2:47). Afterwards, during the days of His ministry, rather often He entered into disputes with the Pharisees and Sadducees (Mark 8:11, 12:28). In the first council of the apostles, much discussion came first, and then the decree was made (Acts 15:7). Augustine testifies about the Church of his day that both lectures and disputations once took place in it (*Epist. 119. ad Januar*). There exists a disputation of Athanasius with Arius that took place before Probus as judge; records of disputations with the Donatists are in the hands of Augustine, and, if I may summarize, there is practically no one among the fathers who did not unsheathe the quill against the heretics of his time. Therefore, we cannot entirely approve what the celebrated Statesman of our time[1] writes, *lib. 4. de Repub. cap. 7.*: "Since religion was once established and confirmed by the consensus of all, lest afterwards it be carried away into disputation, one must beware that all the paths, all the approaches of sedition be cut off and that the bulwarks of peace be fortified. For of whatever matters the disputations are composed on each side, their rationale is both dubious and plausible. And what could be more impious than to use plausible arguments to call into doubt the divine laws, whose nature is eternal and which should inhere in all spirits and minds with a most certain assent? ... What madness is it that exposes the immovable truth of religion to the public disputations of ferocious geniuses and to the impudence of boisterous reason?" These things, I say, we cannot entirely approve and confirm with our vote, much less that which another writes, *Aphorismis Aulicopoliticis Aphor. 289.*: "Let the courtier be the author for the prince, lest he permit public disputations and frequent altercations in the cause of religion, as the kings of the East and of the people of Africa. Even the most perceptive kings of Spain wanted to severely prohibit debates over religions." We certainly admit that distractions of minds, rivalries, and even at times open discord have arisen from disputations over religion. But this happens only by accident, and it is sadly understood that one must bear with the wantonness of men who oppose the truth. Cursed be all concord that is set up against Christ and against the truth! Indeed, it

---

1   Jean Bodin, AD 1530-1596

should not be called concord as much as a foul conspiracy. But for however much, not only the trivial, skirmish-like disputations in the schools, but also the serious battles with the adversaries over the heavenly doctrine, have their uses and their advantages, combined also with a certain necessity, nevertheless it cannot be denied that the same thing happens here which normally happens in other matters of this kind, namely, that the worst abuse occurs with a thing that is good in itself, and the better the thing is, so much worse is the abuse. For many believe that the pinnacle, as it were, of theosophy lies in disputing, while the serious zeal for genuine piety and the more careful cultivation of the inner man are esteemed less. More men would prefer to dispute than to live, as the noble teacher of a terrible student used to say long ago. We, too, can lament over the same thing and in the same way. Many prefer to seek Christ by disputing rather than by imitating His life, although it is better to live in Christ than to seek Him by fighting, as the author to the preface of St. Bernard says. But I say again, by no means are the disputations themselves to be rejected, either the scholastic ones or the ecclesiastical ones. What is to be rejected is the neglect of true and genuine piety, where some think that they have sufficiently discharged their office if they present themselves as vigorous (in their opinion) defenders of the heavenly doctrine, and meanwhile they are sluggish and remiss at imitating the life of Christ and instilling it in the men entrusted to them. Meanwhile, as Gerson teaches (*lib. 4. de consolat. Theol. prosa 4.*), "The theologian must be a good man, educated in the Holy Scriptures, not with an education of the intellect alone, but much more of the disposition, so that he ruminates on the things which he understands by means of theology, applying them to the disposition of the heart and the execution of the work." For who would believe that Christ dwells in that heart which blazes with ambition, burns with hatred, melts with envy? Who will say that such a heart has been purified with true faith, which is still completely contaminated with the filth of avarice and pleasure? We may grant him a knowledge of the letter, but we completely deny him the knowledge of the Spirit. Learn from Me, says Christ, not only that My word is truth (John 17:17), but also that I am meek and humble of heart (Mat. 11:29). I am the way, the truth and the life, He says in John 14:6. Life, because of the merit which is to be embraced with true faith; truth, because of the doctrine which is to be grasped with a believing heart; the way, because of the life which is to be imitated with genuine zeal. He who preaches only the doctrine of Christ and not also His life preaches Christ from only one side." You confess that you know God, but you deny Him with your deeds. Not righteously, but wickedly have you given your tongue to Christ and your soul to the devil," says Bernard (*serm. 24. sup. Cant. Col. 565*). Therefore, let the adversaries be refuted, and refuted sharply by disputations, lectures, and sermons, but let due consideration also be given to temperance, gentleness, and love, which Christ has taught us by His example. Nor do I reject the disciplined and temperate vehemence, summoned in its place, which Augustine explains was used by his Evodius (*Epist. 147. ad Proculian.*): "If, in disputing for his faith and for love of the Church, he has perhaps said something more fervently than your dignity wishes to hear, it should not be called defiance, but confidence. For he wanted to be a contributor and a debater, not a sycophant and a flatterer." At the same time, however, the ministry of righteous rebuke should not be converted into a weapon of madness, about which Augustine warns in *Epist. 174. ad Pascentium*: "As much as possible, let us discuss the divine Scripture peacefully, without contention, not seeking with inane and puerile animosity to be victorious over one another, that the peace of Christ may rather be victorious in our hearts." He writes about himself (*lib. 3. contra literas Petiliani c. 1.*): "When I respond to anyone, either orally or in writing, even if I have been provoked with insulting accusations, as much as the Lord grants me, I look after the hearer or reader, restraining and holding the thorns of vain indignation in check. I do not attempt to make myself superior to the man who insults me. Instead, I seek to be more helpful by refuting his errors." Therefore, far be it from us that in a religious and sacred disputation, we should proceed to insults and political attacks. For here that saying of the Greek Comicus applies: "Rebuke, and be rebuked. But it is not fitting for men who are poets (holy prophets) to revile one another as bread-women." Let there be a pious zeal for truth, on account of which "it is necessary also to take up the household affairs," admonishes the Philosopher (1. *Eth. ad Nicomac. c. 4.*), "that prejudice be shown to no one." Let it be considered "better to be conquered by one who speaks the truth than to conquer one who lies," as Sixtus teaches in *Enchiridio morali ref. vit. Philos. cap. 110*. (But that famous willingness to recant, where is it heard today?) "Let only those things be called under the anvil of disputations which are useful and necessary to know and are defined in the Scriptures. For what good is it to affirm or deny or define with fine distinctions those things which one can go on not knowing without reproach?" Augustine in *Enchirid. ad Laurentium cap. 59.* "It is better to be in doubt about hidden things than to litigate about uncertain things" (Augustine, *lib. 8. de Genes. ad lit. cap. 5*). "The things that God has chosen to hide should not be sought out. But the things which God has made manifest should not be denied, lest we be found unlawfully curious in the former and damnably ungrateful in the latter" (Ambrose, *de vocat. gent. cap. 7*). Consequently, "when a very obscure matter is disputed, something unsupported by certain and clear proofs of the divine Scriptures, then human presumption should restrain itself" (Augustine, *de peccat. merit. lib. 2. cap. ult.*). (If only this had been observed by the Scholastics and were still observed by those who busy themselves with introducing subtle and useless disputations of their own Scholastics into the churches and schools, as if they had a right to return home.

So it seems to Erasmus concerning such men in *Compend. Theolog. pag.* 34., and in *annotat. 1. Tim. 1.*: "Let holy men dispute things in a holy way, not as in the theater of men, but before God and the holy angels, indeed, in the midst of the assembly of the whole Church. And let it be done with zeal, not for contention, but for the truth.") If these and similar conditions are observed, then the disputations will obtain that end for which they were first instituted, and only then will Augustine's famous saying come to fruition, *lib. de nat. et grat. c. 20.*: "O brother, it is good for you to remember that you are a Christian. Perhaps it will be enough to believe these things. And yet, since you wish to dispute, it is not harmful. Indeed, it is even beneficial, if a firm faith leads the way, etc." But if you neglect your prayers, if a zeal for piety is omitted, and you fail to esteem the fear of God as you dispute, the result will be what is found in chapter 25 of the same book: "We are more inclined to ask how we are to respond to those things which are spoken against our error than we are to understand those things which are useful so that we may avoid error. Therefore, with these (adversaries), one must deal, not in disputations as much as in prayers, for them as well as for us." In this sense also the counsel of Sisinnius given to Nectarius, Bishop of Constantinople, is to be understood in Socrates (*lib. 5. Histor. Ecclesiast. c. 10.*), that, "in order to restrain the audacity of heretics, he should avoid dialectic wrangling, and he should summon as witnesses the formulas of faith written by the ancients, for schisms were not settled by quarrels, but even the more pugnacious adversaries avoided them." Therefore, let the abuse be removed, while the true and salutary use of disputations remains untouched. Let us pursue the truth with piety, and piety with truth, for the whole of theology, as defined by the apostle in Titus 1:1, is "the acknowledgment of truth which accords with piety." To this end also I have composed these theological aphorisms, that they might supply the material for pious and peaceful disputation. O courageous man, capable and noble in every way, I chose to write them with due observance for your offspring, with no doubt but that he would find them to be gratifying. Even if everyone preaches against that daily and perpetual zeal which your offspring devotes, to his great credit, to pondering the writings of theologians, and especially the sacred writings, it is far removed from the perverse opinion of those who think that these studies are unsuitable to men of noble birth. But, on the contrary, your offspring thinks it is very noble for his very noble lineage "to learn those things on earth of which the knowledge endures in heaven," and that "the true and holy nobility is that which displays itself in virtues" (and in zeal for piety), as Jerome says, *ad Celanciam*. For this reason, your offspring has obtained for himself a knowledge of theology that is so precise, praiseworthy, and admirable, that whoever hears him speak about sacred matters thinks that he is listening to a professional theologian, as I recall happened to me in Coburg with no small delight. Nor is this a bare and idle knowledge of sacred matters, but it is joined with true and genuine zeal for piety and for all Christian virtues, so that the famous Pindaric can worthily be applied to your offspring, that "he plucks flowers from every virtue." Therefore, O courageous man, capable and most noble in every way, take up these meager scraps which I offer, and continue to embrace me in the future with the same benevolence with which you began, although you can expect nothing in return from my humble state except for vows and prayers. Given at Heldburg on the calends of April, 1611.

Respectfully serving your family,
Johann Gerhard

Chapter 1: Sketch of Theological Headings with their sequence and connection

1. The only proper starting point of theology is the Word of God.

2. For God went forth from the hidden seat of His majesty and manifested Himself to men in His Word.

3. At many times and in many ways, He spoke long ago to the fathers through the prophets, but lately He has spoken to men through His Son (and through the apostles), Heb. 1:1.

4. The prophets and apostles first announced that Word of God with the living voice. Afterward, by the will of God, they condensed the chief and essential parts of divine revelation into the Scriptures. Irenaeus, *lib. 3., cap. 1.*

5. Consequently, the undeniable Word of God cannot be found today anywhere but in the prophetic and apostolic writings.

6. Theology flows from this Word of God and is occupied with it as it sets forth the words of God,[2] Rom. 3:2.

7. It is, therefore, the doctrine of God, from the force of the title, "the word about God."[3]

8. It instructs men, for their salvation, about His essence and will.

9. For this is eternal life, that we should know the true God and Christ the Mediator, sent into the flesh, John 17:3.

10. The question, "Who is God?" unlocks the doctrine of the divine essence, namely, Jehovah Elohim, one in essence, threefold in persons.

---

2 τὰ τοῦ θεοῦ λόγια
3 λόγος περὶ τοῦ θεοῦ

11. For God has manifested Himself in this way, that there are three Persons, neither more nor fewer, in one undivided Essence, namely, the Father, the Son, and the Holy Spirit.

12. The Father is the first Person, not made, nor created, nor begotten, nor proceeding, but unborn and unbegotten.

13. The Son is the second Person, not made, nor created, but begotten of the Father from eternity.

14. In the fullness of time, He took on a human nature, in which and through which He paid the price of our redemption.

15. The Holy Spirit is the third Person, not made, nor created, nor begotten, but proceeding from the Father and the Son from eternity.

16. The will of God must be considered from the decrees made from eternity.

17. The two main decrees are: the decree of creation and of restoration; of creation and of re-creation; of formation and of reformation.

18. The execution of those decrees in time demonstrates the nature of those decrees.

19. For what God does and how He acts in time, that He decreed to do and in that way to act from eternity.

20. The rationale for this statement depends on the immutability of the divine will.

21. Creation was done in time; it is the manifestation of the decree that was made from eternity concerning the creation of all things.

22. It consists in the production of angels, of men, and of the rest of the created things, in the first six days of the world, by God the Father, through the Son, in the Holy Spirit, for His glory.

23. A large number of the angels turned away from God; the rest, having been confirmed in goodness, honor God and serve men.

24. The first two human beings, at the instigation of Satan, likewise transgressed the divine Law, which had been engraved on their hearts and made known by the divine voice.

25. In this way, then, the image of God in them was wiped out by that fall, and their nature was corrupted by sin.

26. Consequently, their descendants were and are born destitute of original righteousness and miserably corrupted by sin.

27. By this disease of sin, all the powers of the soul have been so corrupted in man that only the faint light of reason and the feeble powers of the will have remained in external matters.

28. This fall of the first-formed could not escape the notice of the omniscient God. Therefore, out of immense mercy, on account of the intercession of the Son, He made the decree from eternity concerning the restoration of men.

29. The nature of that decree is likewise demonstrated by the execution of the decree; in time, He sent the Son to be the Redeemer and Mediator. Therefore, He decreed from eternity to send Him.

30. Through the word, He offers to all people the benefits of the Mediator and applies them to believers. Therefore, He decided from eternity to offer those benefits to all people through the word and to apply them to believers.

31. In the Scriptures, this decree is called election and predestination, concerning which no judgment is to be made except *a posteriori*, that is, from its manifestation.

32. We observe in the execution of this decree that God set forth the Word and Sacraments for the restoration of man.

33. The Word is summed up in two chief parts: the Law and the Gospel.

34. The Law is the doctrine of works. Therefore, it shows the corruption of nature, it terrifies, and it prescribes the standard of doing good.

35. The Gospel is the doctrine of faith. It points to Christ the Mediator, who made satisfaction for sins, and it cheers a man's conscience.

36. The praxis of Law and Gospel consists in true repentance.

37. Therefore, repentance has two parts: contrition, which comes from the Law; and faith, which comes from the Gospel.

38. Faith lays hold of the righteousness of Christ, which has been offered in the Word of the Gospel. Through faith, the man who has first been crushed by the voice of the Law is justified before God and, having received at the same time the Holy Spirit, begins to be renewed.

39. For hearts are purified by faith (Acts 15:9).

40. The fruits of true repentance, then, are good works.

41. For faith, indeed, is efficacious through love (Gal. 5:6), and Christ gives us, not only His righteousness, but also the Holy Spirit who begins to renew our nature and to restrain the lusts of the flesh.

42. There are three classes of good works, for some good works have God in view, others have us in view, and still others, the neighbor.

43. For the sum of godliness is this, that we should live godly, righteously, and soberly (Titus 2:12).

44. The Sacraments are seals of the Word. Therefore, they were instituted for confirming faith. They are the visible Word.

45. The Sacraments in the Old Testament are circumcision and the Paschal Lamb; in the New, Baptism and the Lord's Supper.

46. By that Word, both heard and seen, the Church on this earth is gathered to God.

47. There are three hierarchies of the Church: the ecclesiastical, the political, and the domestic.

48. The Roman pope wants to be the monarch and head of the ecclesiastical hierarchy.

49. But since he wants to be in the place of Christ[4] without divine appointment, he thus becomes the Antichrist.

50. The ministry of the Word, that is, the ecclesiastical hierarchy, is established today through a mediate call.

51. The political hierarchy is composed of magistrates, both lower and higher.

52. To the domestic hierarchy belongs marriage, which is, as it were, the nursery of the Church.

53. In this life, God subjects His Church to the cross, for which He has the most pressing reasons.

54. He will, at last, glorify the Church in the coming life, when it is liberated and free from all enemies, evils and dangers.

55. For the godly and believing, death and the last judgment are the portal to eternal life, without any intermediate purgatory.

56. But the wicked and unbelieving will finally be cast into the inextinguishable fire of hell.

---

[4] αντὶ χριστοῦ

18

Chapter 2: The Holy Scripture

1. The only starting point of theology is the Word of God as it has been set forth today in the sacred documents.

2. With the title 'Holy Scripture,' properly and strictly speaking, we understand the Old and New Testament books that are unquestionably prophetic and apostolic.

3. They are also called 'canonical,' since they are the fullest canon and rule of divine knowledge and worship.

4. These are the canonical books in the Old Testament: Genesis, Exodus, Leviticus, Numbers, Deuteronomy, Joshua, Judges, Ruth, 1 & 2 Samuel, 1 & 2 Kings, 1 & 2 Chronicles, Ezra, Nehemiah, Esther, Job, Psalms, Proverbs, Ecclesiastes, Song of Songs, Isaiah, Jeremiah, Lamentations, Ezekiel, Daniel, Hosea, Joel, Amos, Obadiah, Jonah, Micah, Nahum, Habakkuk, Zephaniah, Haggai, Zechariah, Malachi.

5. The rest of the Old Testament books are ecclesiastical (Jerome calls them 'Apocryphal'); they were neither written by the prophets nor considered canonical by the Jewish Church.

6. They also lack the testimony of Christ and the apostles.

7. Moreover, they are considered to be outside the canon by the most esteemed councils and fathers.

8. In addition, it can be demonstrated that most of them contain things that either clearly disagree with the canonical books, or that overturn the historical and chronological truth, or that contradict themselves.

9. The books of the New Testament are called 'canonical' which have always been received as truly and certainly apostolic by all the Churches without any doubt.

10. They are: the Gospels of Matthew, Mark, Luke and John, the Acts of the Apostles, the Epistle of Paul to the Romans, 1 & 2 Corinthians, Galatians, Ephesians, Philippians, Colossians, 1 & 2 Thessalonians, 1 & 2 Timothy, Titus, Philemon, 1 Peter, 1 John.

11. The rest were once not received by all with such a consensus of judgment, and in this respect, they are called 'apocryphal' by some.

12. They are: the Epistle to the Hebrews, James, 2 Peter, 2 & 3 John, Jude, the Revelation of John.

13. But since most of the fathers did not really doubt concerning their primary author, namely, the Holy Spirit, but only concerning the secondary authors, therefore we gladly allow them to be made equal to the canonical books with regard to their authority to test doctrine, nor will we fight with anyone over this matter.

14. The Holy Scripture is inspired by God (2 Tim. 3:16). Therefore, the holy men of God did not only speak, but also wrote by the impulse of the Holy Spirit (2 Pet. 3:21).

15. The same Word of God which was announced and preserved without the Scripture through the living voice, for a very long time in the Old Testament, and for not such a long period of time in the New—the same Word, I say, was later written down through the will of God in the Scriptures. (Irenaeus, *lib. 3., cap. 1.*)

16. Therefore, we do not allow any real difference to be established between the preached Word of God and the written Word.

17. For it is suitable for the Word of God either to be preached or to be written.

18. But while it is true that the prophets and apostles, as they were carried along by the Holy Spirit, did not write down their entire sermons, nevertheless the things they chose to write were the things that seemed sufficient for the salvation of believers (Augustine, *tract. 49. in Johan.*).

19. Therefore, we say that the Holy Scripture is perfect, that is, it contains all the things that are necessary for instilling faith and for setting a pattern for life to those who are contending for the prize of eternal life.

20. The clear testimony of this perfection is set forth in 2 Tim. 3:16–17, where Holy Scripture is said to be so useful for instruction, reproof, correction, and training that the man of God may be perfect, equipped for every good work. Therefore, the Scripture can also make us wise for salvation.

21. Therefore, since there is a twofold use understood in relation to a need—adequate and complete, that is, sufficient, removing everything that is lacking; and partial, which removes what is lacking, not alone, but with other helpers—it is clear that the apostle is speaking specifically about the first use.

22. From the things that have been written, we can learn faith in Christ (John 20:31), and be equipped for every good work (2 Tim. 3:17), and the brothers of the rich man could have escaped the torments of hell by hearing Moses and the prophets in the Scriptures (Luke 16:29).

23. This perfection that we assign to the Scriptures follows naturally, for he who believes in Christ, he who is equipped for every good work, and he who becomes a partaker of eternal life—what more will he desire?

24. This argument must also be considered: the apostle Paul announced to the Church at Ephesus the whole counsel of God, namely, concerning our salvation (Acts 20:27). The same apostle said nothing apart from Moses and the prophets (Acts 26:22). Therefore, the whole counsel of God concerning our salvation is contained in Moses and the prophets.

25. But if the Scripture is perfect, then farewell to those traditions which, besides the Scripture, are introduced to be taken up with the same affection of godliness and faith.

26. For they are of doubtful credibility, they are often self-contradictory, they are extremely subject to corruptions of the truth.

27. Church history testifies that, in the early Church, falsehoods were devised under the name of apostolic traditions, and that the notion of tradition also deceived many men long ago.

28. Furthermore, since the Holy Scripture was presented to men by God Himself for this purpose, that they should be taught from it for salvation, therefore we conclude that the Scripture is perspicuous.

29. Is God, the Maker of the mind and the tongue, unable to speak clearly? On the contrary, with great providence, He wanted the things that are divine to be free of disguise, so that all might understand the things which He was saying to all (Lactantius, *lib.* 6. *div. Instit. c. 21.*).

30. Is it not supposed to educate, that is, to make a wise and learned man out of an uneducated and ignorant one? Then it must be perspicuous.

31. It is perspicuity that teaches, not obscurity or perplexity.

32. Furthermore, when we say that the Holy Scripture is perspicuous, we certainly do not mean that all the things set forth in the Scriptures are arranged in such a way that they are obvious to everyone at first glance.

33. But we mean that the perspicuity of Scripture is such that, from it, one can obtain a certain and dependable judgment concerning the dogmas which a person must know to be saved.

34. The whole of Scripture is made up of the prophetic and the apostolic Word. But there are testimonies concerning the perspicuity of them both. How, then, could it be determined that whole Scripture is obscure?

35. The prophetic Word set forth in the Old Testament is compared to a lamp (Psalm 119:105). In 2 Pet. 1:19, the same is said of the apostolic Word. In 2 Cor. 4:3–4, that which is obscure and hidden by accident must, *per se*, by its own nature, be perspicuous.

36. From the demonstrated perfection and perspicuity of Scripture, it follows that it is the certain and only standard in the controversies which are stirred up concerning the chief headings of the Christian religion.

37. What is said in Psalm 19:5 about the apostles, that "their line," that is, their plumb line, "has gone out into all the earth," Paul applies in Rom. 10:18 to the doctrine of the apostles. But the apostles wrote and taught the same things.

38. Christ, too, and the apostles, in settling controversies of faith, never appealed nor sent us running to any other standard but the Scripture. What lamb will not follow these doctors and pastors?

39. The Word of Christ, of the prophets and of the apostles contained in the Holy Scripture will judge all people on the last day (John 12:48, Rom. 2:16, Rev. 20:12). What, then, keeps it from being the standard—yes, even the perfect standard—in this life?

40. For if some part of the heavenly doctrine has been set forth apart from the canonical books, how will the whole judgment take place from them?

41. Furthermore, since it has not only been granted, but also commanded to all Christians to test the spirits (1 John 4:1); to beware of false prophets (Mat. 7:15); to test all things (1 The. 5:21); it is for this reason incumbent upon them to discern the divine truth from human dreams. Indeed, the standard of that truth, namely, the Scripture, will pertain to all, and thus the laity are not to be prevented from reading the Scripture.

42. What the Holy Spirit approves and commends, no one should call forbidden. But the Bereans are commended for this very thing, that they examined Paul's sermon by the Scriptures (Acts 17:11); the elect pilgrims of the dispersion in Pontus, Galatia, Cappadocia, Asia, and Bithynia are commended, because they were in the habit of attending to the prophetic Word as to a lamp (2 Pet. 1:19); the diligent study of the Scriptures is commended to all

Christians (Col. 3:16).

43. And although the laity are mostly ignorant of the Hebrew and Greek languages in which the Old and New Testaments were written, and yet they should still read the Scripture, therefore the zeal of those who translated the Holy Scriptures into the vernacular is not to be disapproved.

44. And yet only the Hebrew text in the Old Testament and the Greek text in the New are original, for these, of course, are the languages in which each Testament was written.

45. That which departs from those fountains neither can nor should be considered any longer the prophetic and apostolic Word, since it is not inspired by God.

46. Therefore, that Vulgate edition which can be more easily claimed than proven to be Jerome's work, cannot by any right be exalted to the throne of original authority.

47. Indeed, it has many typographical, elliptic, chronographic, and dogmatic errors.

48. Those who claim that the Hebrew text is corrupt have a corrupt mind.

49. Nor do they love the pure truth who deny that the fountains flow purely.

50. The end and benefit of Holy Scripture is obtained through the legitimate interpretation of the same.

51. But since the Scripture is perfect and perspicuous, therefore it is to be interpreted from itself and by itself.

52. For that which is perfect should have no need of a heterogeneous patch; that which is perspicuous needs no foreign light.

53. Although the Scripture is perspicuous, the eyes of our darkened mind see its light poorly.

54. Therefore, let the one who is about to attempt the interpretation of Scripture plead with heartfelt groans that his mind may be enlightened by the Holy Spirit.

55. Let the glory of God and the equipping of men for salvation be the supreme law of interpretation.

56. And since every chapter whatsoever of heavenly doctrine has been explained somewhere in the Scripture with proper and perspicuous words, let the interpretation of the rest of the passages be in conformity with those; thus it will be analogous to the faith (Rom. 12:6).

57. Let him carefully observe the native meanings of the vocables.

58. In dubious matters, let him make haste to the Hebrew fountains in the Old Testament and to the Greek fountains in the New.

59. Let the aim of every saying, the circumstances, and the things that come before and after, be studiously kept in view.

60. Let the things that are fewer and more obscure be explained by the things that are clearer and more abundant.

61. Let no one turn back from a single letter, especially in the articles of faith, unless the Scripture itself shows the impropriety and explains it.

62. Let a person skillfully use the writings of the fathers as a tool and a guide in the interpretation of Scripture.

63. Meanwhile, let no one hold these writings to be canonical, but let him consider them on the basis of the canonical writings. Whatever in them agrees with the authority of the divine Scriptures, let him accept with the fathers' approval. Whatever does not agree, let him spit out with their blessing (Augustine, *lib. 2. contra Cresc. cap. 32.*).

Chapter 3: God

1. The highest goal of the entire Scripture is the knowledge of God, and after that, the worship of Him.

2. All things flow from that one goal, to that one goal.

3. Even the book of nature shows that God exists, for the world is the school of the knowledge of God (Basil *in Hexaem.*).

4. There are mainly three pages in this book: Heaven, Earth, Sea, and all that is in them, as Clement of Alexandria says.

5. But from the book of Holy Scripture the more certain, more apparent, and more perfect knowledge of God can be sought.

6. The eyes of our mind were darkened through the Fall, which is why we are able to progress less expeditiously in the book of nature.

7. The goal of that natural knowledge of God is "to seek God," as the apostle says (Acts 17:27).

8. Nature itself testifies of its own imperfection. Therefore, there should be a guide for finding the fuller revelation in the Church.

9. The essence of God transcends all created things. Therefore, the perfect knowledge of Him also transcends all understanding, the "divine incomprehensible" (Damascenus, *1. orth. fid. c. 1.*).

10. Consequently, just as that highest Spirit (God) cannot be properly imagined by any intellect, so He cannot be properly defined or limited by any limitation (Augustine, *de cogn. verae vitae, cap. 7.*).

11. By no expressions can He be understood to have been so fully revealed as by those which set forth our ignorance (Scal., *exerc. 365. sect. 2.*).

12. Therefore, the things which God has desired to remain hidden are not to be investigated; nevertheless, the things which He has made manifest by the revelation of Himself are not to be neglected, lest we be found illicitly curious in the former and damnably ungrateful in the latter (Ambrose, *1. de vocat. gent. c. 7.*).

13. God has given all things their being; therefore, He is the first, highest, and independent Being.

14. He exists of Himself[5] (Scal., as previously cited); the super-essential Essence[6] (Dionys., *lib. 1. de div. nomin. cap. 1.*).

15. He is the Essence of all essences, the Creator of all creatures, the Life of all the living, the Cause of all causes.

16. He Himself gives all things to all and receives nothing from any.

17. There is nothing above Him; nothing outside of Him; nothing without Him; nothing below Him. Everything is under Him; everything in Him; everything with Him. All things are from Him, all things through Him, all things in Him (Augustine, *de Specul. c. 33.*).

18. The essence of God and the essence of creatures are separated by an infinite difference; essence applies to God uniquely and specially.

19. God is spirit (John 4:24). A spirit does not have flesh and bones (Luke 24:39). Therefore, God is incorporeal.

20. The corporeal things that are attributed to God anthropopathically[7] are to be understood in a manner fit for God[8].

21. God comes down to us so that we might rise up to Him; and since we are men, He speaks to us in the customary human way.

22. The Scripture teaches spiritual things by means of bodily things; it teaches invisible things by means of visible things.

---

5 αὐταυτός
6 οὐσία ὑπερούσιος
7 ἀνθρωποπαθῶς
8 θεοπρέπως

23. Thus God is said to have eyes, which are on the righteous; a hand, by which He gives food to all flesh; feet, of which the earth is the footstool. He has all these things by way of effect, not by way of condition (Bernard, *serm. 4. sup. Cant.*).

24. He is, therefore, all eye, for He sees all things; all hand, for He works all things; all foot, for He is everywhere (Augustine, *on Psa. 136.*).

25. He is the eternal God, without beginning or end; all things are from Him; He Himself is from nothing; He is not subject to any change or succession; He alone can say, "I am who I am, I will be who I will be" (Exo. 3:6).

26. If a beginning were attributed to God, then change would also have to be attributed to Him; He is uncreated, timeless, without beginning, without end, ageless. Therefore, He is truly eternal.

27. But if He is without change, then He is also certainly without composition of any kind.

28. He alone is truly and properly simple; all things except for Him are composed, if not otherwise, then at least of act and energy, of being and essence.

29. The essence of God is not only simple, but also infinite and immense; God aids all things, not only by His power, with which He preserves all things, but also by His essence, with which He is more intimately present with the created things than they are with themselves.

30. In those words in which God is said to be present everywhere essentially, one should believe that more is contained than living man is able to grasp (Lombard, *1. sent. dist. 37. f.*).

31. Nevertheless, God is not extended throughout local spaces like a corporeal mass, so that one half of Him is in one half of the physical world, and the other half in the other, and in this way, by summing up the total, He is whole; but He is whole in heaven

alone and whole on earth alone and not bound by any location; He is whole everywhere in Himself (Augustine, *Epist. 57. ad Dard.*).

32. Nor on that account is He mixed in with things or contaminated with the filth of things. He is within all created things, but not included in them; He is outside all created things, but not excluded from them.

33. The goodness, wisdom, and power of God are understood from an inspection of the created things; the mercy, righteousness, and truth of God are understood from His administration of the world. For this reason, the more prudent among the heathen have acknowledged these things.

34. In the book of Scripture, the testimonies about these and other attributes of God are greater in number, heavier in weight, clearer in perspicuity.

35. But since God is immutable, these attributes are not qualities in God, but they are the very essence of God. Wisdom is not something added on top of the divine essence, but is the essence itself.

36. There is nothing in God that is not God Himself (Bernard, *serm. 80. sup. Cant.*).

37. Therefore, let us understand God, if we are able, as much as we are able, to be good without quality, great without quantity, as creating without need, as presenting without position, as holding all things together without posture, as whole in every place without place, as eternal without time, making changeable things without any change of Himself, and undergoing nothing (Augustine, *5. de Trin. c. 1.*).

38. The Catholic Church, taught by God Himself in the Scriptures, believes and professes that there is one true God.

39. The Trinity of Persons is not at odds with this most united (so to speak) unity of the divine Essence; the one true God is Father, Son, and Holy Spirit.

40. We say three Persons, but without prejudice toward the

unity in Essence; we say one God, but without confusion of the Trinity (Bernard, *lib. 5. ad Eugen. in princ.*).

41. Do you ask how this can be? Let it suffice for you to believe that it is so; it is temerity to investigate this outside the limitations of the Word; it is godliness to believe; it is eternal life to know (Bernard, in the place cited.).

42. The being of the Father is the being of the Son and the being of the Holy Spirit, but to be the Father is not to be the Son, nor to be the Holy Spirit.

43. I and the Father are one, says the Son (John 10:30). He said "one" with respect to the unity of Essence, and His saying frees you from Arius. He said "We are" with respect to the distinction of Persons, and His saying frees you from Sabellius (Augustine, *lib. 5. de Trin. cap. 9.*).

44. We should neither think of God as one without wrapping Him in the radiance of the three Persons; nor should we distinguish the three Persons without being drawn at once to the one God (Nazianzenus, *serm. de sacro Bapt.*).

45. Let us believe one Divinity without a distinct separation of confusion, so that each Person is not considered in Trinity, nor three substances in unity; but let a plurality be assigned to the unity in such a way that equality is not subtracted from the Trinity (Augustine, *serm. 29. de tempore.*).

46. The Father was made by no one, nor created, nor begotten, nor proceeding. The Son was not made, nor created, but begotten of the Father alone; the Holy Spirit was not made, nor created, nor begotten, but proceeds from the Father and the Son (Athanasius in the Creed.).

47. The term 'diversity' must be avoided in divine matters, lest the unity of Essence be removed; the term 'separation' or 'division' must be avoided, lest the simplicity of the divine Essence be removed; the term 'disparity' must be avoided, lest the equality of Per-

sons be removed; the terms 'foreign' and 'differing' must be avoided, lest the sameness of the Essence be removed; the term 'singularity' must be avoided, lest the one Deity that is common to the three be undermined.

48. The term 'single' must be avoided, lest the number of Persons be removed; the term 'co-mingled' must be avoided, lest the order of Persons be removed; the term 'solitary' must be avoided, lest the fellowship of the three Persons be removed (*Th. p. 1. q. 31. art. 2.*).

49. We should not say with Zanchius that the three Persons are essential parts of God (*lib. 2. de trib. Elohim c. 7. p. 529.*).

50. Augustine's judgment is better, that the Essence, made up of Father, Son, and Holy Spirit, is proclaimed, not as a genus made up of species, nor as species made up of individuals, nor as a whole made up of parts, but in a certain other ineffable and incomprehensible way.

51. Nor should we say with Calvin (*lib. 1. Instit. cap. 13. sect. 23*) and with Zanchius (*lib. 1. de trib. Eloh. c. 3*) and likewise with Sohnius (*tom. 2. Exeg. p. 123.*) that the Father is God according to His prominence.

52. For where the sameness of the Essence is, there is no prominence or inequality. Here one must speak purely and cautiously.

53. Nor should the eternity of the Son be denied because He was begotten of the Father, since He was begotten from eternity.

54. The eternal Father generates the eternal Son.

55. The generation of the Son should be understood to have been done impassibly, timelessly, without fluctuation, inseparably (Damascenus, *lib. 1. orth. fid. c. 8.*).

56. Nevertheless, it is properly called a 'generation.' The Word is properly the Son of God the Father, and therefore is truly and properly begotten of the Father.

57. But observe, both here and elsewhere, that whatever things are transferred from the created things to God must first

be purged of all imperfections, and only then should that which is perfect be attributed to God (Zanch., *7. de trib. Eloh. c. 7.*).

58. The sayings of the fathers, that the Son went forth from the mind of the Father, are not to be hatefully attacked; they meant to denote the impassibility of the generation (Nazianzenus, *orat. 2. de Filio. Basil. sup. 1. Joh.*).

59. Nor, however, should these things be stretched, but they should be explained piously.

60. To discuss the Persons worthily transcends the power of reason; what it means to be begotten, what it means to have proceeded exceeds our natural abilities. I have professed that I do not know (Rob. Holcoth. *q. 10. determinationum*, cited by Biel, *1. sent. dist. 13. q. un.*).

61. Let us put together a definition: God is a spiritual, simple, intelligent, eternal, true, good, righteous, holy, pure, merciful, entirely free Being of immense wisdom and power, different from the created things and all the bodies of the world. The eternal Father, who, from eternity, from His own Essence, begot the Son as His substantial image; and the Son, who is the coeternal image of the Father, begotten of the Father from eternity; and the Holy Spirit, proceeding from the Father and the Son, is the Creator and Preserver of all things, the Redeemer and Sanctifier of the Church, one true God, blessed forever.

62. In summary, God is Jehovah Elohim, that is, one divine Essence of three Persons. The Holy Trinity is the undivided unity of three.

Chapter 4: The Person and Office of Christ

1. The explanation of the doctrine concerning Christ should be as pleasing to us as the knowledge of Christ the Savior is salutary.

2. Christ is the God-Man[9], true God and true Man.

3. It is equally dangerous to deny either the Divinity or the flesh of our body in Christ.

4. He is God through the eternal generation from the Father; He is Man through the assumption of flesh from Mary.

5. For the Word did not carry His flesh down from heaven with Him, but took up the true human nature from the purified blood of Mary.

6. That assumption exceeds the entire course of nature, indeed, the entire grasp of our mind, for it was done by the special working of the Holy Spirit.

7. But in this case the Holy Spirit of God did not act seminally, but creatively.

8. It exceeds the limits of nature for a virgin to conceive without the seed of a male; for a virgin to be the mother of a most holy birth, indeed, to be the one who gives birth to God. But it does not place limits on the work of the Holy Spirit.

9. The Word assumed, not only a true human nature, but also a whole human nature, that is, both perfect and free from all defect of sin.

10. But He assumed it into the unity of His Person, and thus the assumption of flesh is the personal union itself of the Word and the flesh.

---

[9] θεάνθρωπος

11. The Person did not assume a person, but the second Person of the Trinity assumed a human nature.

12. Therefore, there is not one who is God and another who is Man in Christ; but the same one is God who is also Man.

13. Not one person and another person, but one thing and another thing is in Christ.

14. Indeed, the duality of natures should be affirmed in such a way that the most intimate and indissoluble unity of person is not denied.

15. The fathers say that only the Person of the Son was incarnate.

16. In saying this, the word 'Person' is not being contrasted with the divine nature of the Son, but with the Person of the Father and the Holy Spirit.

17. For they say elsewhere, and rightly so, that the entire Divinity was incarnate in one of its own Persons[10].

18. The Person of the Word and the divine nature of the Word are not, in reality, different.

19. The Divinity is whole and perfect in each Person.

20. Therefore, since one Person was incarnate, it is rightly said that the whole Divinity was incarnate; namely, in the one Person of the Word.

21. The union of the divine and human natures in Christ is personal, but not of persons; it is the union of natures, but not natural.

22. It is also an inseparable union with respect to both time and place.

23. For the Word will never set aside the flesh which He once assumed.

24. He certainly does not set aside the nature which He once united to Himself.

---

10   ἐν μίᾳ τῶν ἑαυτῆς ὑποστάσεων

25. The human nature which He assumed is not independently inhering, nor self-subsisting, nor un-subsisting, but in-subsisting.[11]

26. It is in-subsisting, not by any sort of gestation in the Word, but by the fullest communion of the whole Person of the Word.

27. Therefore, after the incarnation took place, the Person of the Word should not be considered apart from the flesh, nor the flesh apart from the Person of the Word.

28. What God has joined together, what has been joined together in God, let man neither separate nor rend asunder.

29. Nor should the bare circumstance[12] of the united natures be considered, but rather the close and most intimate interpenetration[13].

30. When describing the union of the Person, the fathers say that the union was made indivisibly, inseparably, without intermission.[14]

31. When describing the duality of natures, they say that the union was made without confusion, without change, without transmutation, without conversion.[15]

32. The flesh remains finite in the union itself, and so no equalization or coextension of the natures takes place.

33. Through the union, the flesh becomes a partaker of the infinite Person, and so no separation of the natures takes place through intervals of locations.

34. On account of this personal union, it is rightly said that the Son of God is the Son of Mary; and the corollary, that the Son of Mary is the Son of God. God is man, and man is God.

35. These propositions are most conveniently referred to as 'personal.'

---

11 non est ἰδιοσύστατος, nec αὐθυπόστατος, nec ἀνυπόστατος, sed ἐνυπόστατος
12 περίστασις
13 περιχώρησις
14 ἀδιαιρέτως, ἀχωρίστως, ἀδιαστάτως
15 ἀσυγχύτως, ἀτρέπτως, ἀναλλοιώτως, ἀμεταβλήτως

36. For their foundation consists in the personal union, and their entire force, truth, propriety, and connection should be considered from the personal union of the two natures in Christ.

37. These propositions neither can nor should be subjected to the rules of logic, since the incarnation of the Word exceeds human—and even angelic—words.

38. Therefore, these are not regular propositions, since they rise above reason and logic.

39. And yet they should not be taken figuratively, since the Son of God is the Son of Man, not in a figurative way, but truly and properly.

40. The consequence of the personal union is the communication of attributes.

41. For since the Deity and the attributes of the Deity are the same thing, and since humanity has its attributes closely related to the nature, therefore the union of the divine and human natures in Christ implies a certain communication of attributes.

42. First, those two natures do not subsist separately, but are united in one Person.

43. Therefore, each nature does not do alone and by itself the things which are proper to each one, but the Person does all things according to the character of each nature.

44. Therefore, the properties of one nature are attributed to the Person in a concrete sense.

45. The fathers call this a mutual attribution, a mode of mutual attribution, and most helpfully, appropriation.[16]

46. The name 'Person' is always placed as the subject of these propositions in order to vindicate the unity of the Person.

47. Whenever they are expressly added in the predicate, the distinctive particles are always implicitly understood in order to affirm the distinct character of the natures.

---

16   ἀντίδοσις, τρόπος ἀντιδόσεως, ἰδιοποιία

48. Those propositions are reciprocal; that is, the divine is proclaimed of the human, just as the human is proclaimed of the divine.

49. For it is an equal union; the human nature is as intimately united to the divine as the divine is to the human.

50. The Son of Man is the Creator of heaven and earth. The Son of God suffered. Both sayings are entirely correct.

51. Creation does not apply to the assumed humanity by condition of the nature, but it is still correctly attributed to the Son of Man on account of the sameness of the Person.

52. In the same way, suffering does not apply to the Divinity by condition of the nature, but, nonetheless, it pertains to the Son of God on account of the intimate and ineffable union of natures, as if He had sustained it in His own divine nature itself.

53. Indeed, by assuming the human nature in the unity of the Person, the Word appropriated all His attributes to Himself personally.

54. Vigilius says this (*lib. 2. contra Eut.*): God did not suffer in the character of the nature, but in the unity of the Person.

55. Secondly, the personal union was made on account of His office as Mediator.

56. In this office, the one nature is not lazily resting, or off doing its own things by itself, or doing something different from the other nature, but both natures act in communion with the other.

57. Therefore, the names of the office apply to Christ and are proclaimed about Christ according to both natures.

58. For the actions of both natures come together for a common purpose[17], and a *theanthropic* or divine-human action is done.

59. The fathers call it 'communication' and 'periphrasis.'[18]

60. Thirdly, in the office of Mediator, the human nature does not do only human things, but since it has been enriched with

---

17 ἀποτέλεσμα
18 κοινοποιία καὶ περίφρασις

the divine functions on account of its pure union to the Word, therefore it is and is called the instrument[19] of the Deity, not separated or divided, but personally united, in which, with which, and through which the Word acts in the office of Mediator (Damascenus, 3. *Orth. fid. cap. 17.*).

61. Since the divine nature in Christ is already completely perfect, it is not enriched with anything in that union. But a great addition has been made to the human nature, since besides, above, and beyond its own essential properties, which it retains forever, it has obtained divine advantages in and from that personal union.

62. The fathers call this 'exaltation, glorification, sharing in the divine degrees, impartation' and 'participation in the divine powers, improvement, richness, ascent.'[20]

63. Scripture clearly testifies, and the godly fathers approve with great consensus, that the conferring of those advantages has taken place according to the human nature of Christ.

64. Therefore, when such things are said to be conferred on the Son by the Father in time, they are to be understood as having been conferred according to the human nature.

65. That there may be a relationship between the Father who gives and the Son who receives in time, not with respect to the divine nature, according to which He is essentially one with the Father; and whatever the Father does, He does likewise (John 5:10); but with respect to the human nature, which was fit for, and in need of, them.

66. Truly infinite and immense are the gifts that have been given; namely, all authority, divine glory, all the treasures of wisdom, life-giving power, authority to judge, the present rule over heaven and earth.

67. And yet one should not imagine or consider here a physical outpouring of the divine attributes, but as the union itself is personal, so also is the communication.

19   *organum*
20   ὑπερύψασις, δόξασις, μετάληψις θείας ἀξίας, μετάδοσις καὶ μετοχὴ θείας ἐξουσίας, βελτίωσις, πλοῦτος, ἀνάβασις

68. The Divinity of the Word suffered no loss of its attributes, nor did those attributes become proper to the flesh through this communication.

69. But the divine nature of the Son, retaining its own attributes within the most intimate encircling of its person, and nonetheless assuming the human nature into the communion and unity of its Person, assumed it at once into a communion of attributes; that is, it stretches out its attributes in, with, and through the human nature as its personal organ.

70. Therefore, the basis of that communication properly consists in assumption.[21]

71. For the human nature did not assume the divine, but the Word is the assuming Person; the human nature is assumed in and by His Person.

72. The union of natures is equal, but in that union, it belongs to the Word to assume, while it belongs to the flesh to be assumed.

73. Consequently, even though the union of natures is equal, nevertheless the condition of the united natures is unequal.

74. I do not claim that the Deity was affected by the injury to His body, as we know that the flesh was glorified by the majesty of the Deity.

75. Finally, since that communication is an essential result of the union, it certainly took place in the first moment of the incarnation.

76. Nevertheless, the state of exinanition intervened for us and for our salvation.

77. For in order that Christ our Mediator might be able to suffer and die, He did not fully reveal in the days of His flesh the glory and majesty that were communicated to Him according to the human nature.

78. He did not reveal it, I say, but at the same time He did not completely lack it; He emptied Himself, not by a complete set-

---

21 πρόσληψις

ting aside of His glory and power, but by withdrawing their use and manifest splendor.

79. To this state of exinanition pertain His conception, gestation in the womb, nativity, growth in age and wisdom, obedience in the form of a servant up to the death of the cross, followed by His burial.

80. Christ's exinanition was followed by His glorious exaltation, to which pertain the descent into hell, the resurrection from the dead, the ascension into heaven, and the session at the right hand of God.

81. All these things pertain to the office of Mediator, on account of which the wondrous union of the divine and human natures was made, and which Christ administers according to both natures.

82. The diversity of natures in Christ and the unity of the Person availed for this office, so that if the human nature was unable to do what needed to be done for the restoration of men, the divine nature might do it; and if something were not at all fitting for the divine nature, the human nature might provide it.

83. So that it might not be one and the other, but the same one who, existing perfectly in both natures, might pay through the human nature what it owed, and might be able to do through the divine nature what was expedient (Anselm, 2. *Cur Deus homo. cap. 18.*).

84. A mere man could not make satisfaction; God owed nothing. Therefore, God became man, so that He who owed nothing for Himself might be able to make satisfaction for us.

85. Christ executes this office of Mediator in such a way that He is our Prophet, Priest, and King.

86. The prophetic office consists in the revelation of the Gospel and in the institution and preservation of the ministry.

87. The parts of the priestly office are satisfaction and intercession.

88. The kingdom of Christ is considered either according to this life or the next.

89. In this life, it is a kingdom of power or of grace. The former is the general rule over all things, while the latter consists in the special works of grace in the Church.

90. In the next life, it will be a kingdom of glory, into which all the elect will one day be received after they are raised from the dust, of which Christ our King, forever blessed, makes us partakers.

Chapter 5: Creation and the Angels

1. God, who is invisible by nature, in order that He might be known to those who are visible, made a certain work, that it might manifest the Workman by its visibility (Ambrose, *in cap. 1. Rom.*).

2. This temporal act of God is and is called 'creation.'

3. It is nothing other than the production of the entire universe, by the Father, through the Son, in the Holy Spirit, in six distinct days, from nothing, for the glory of God Himself, and for the salvation of men.

4. Therefore, the Author of creation is God, one in Essence, three in Persons.

5. Moreover, the creation of all things is the immediate act of God alone.

6. The Father created by speaking, which the Evangelist teaches is to be taken about the personal and consubstantial Word of God (John 1:1, 9).

7. The Spirit of the Lord was brooding over the waters (Gen. 1:2), which the Psalm shows is to be taken about the Spirit of His mouth, that it, about the personal and consubstantial Spirit of God (Psalm 33:6).

8. Therefore, when Moses calls the Creator 'Elohim,' he is most correctly referring to the Trinity of Persons.

9. When you hear that the Father created all things, through the Son, in the Holy Spirit, be careful that you do not take this to refer to an inequality of essence or power in performing the action.

10. For whatever the Father does, the Son does likewise (John 5:19).

11. But this whole matter should be related to the real distinction of Persons, and, as a result, to the classification of acts in works on the outside[22].

12. Therefore, the Father created through the Son, not as if through an idle or separate instrument, but as through the coeternal image which is consubstantial to Him.

13. Moreover, He created all things out of nothing.

14. Some things, of course, He created immediately, others mediately (Damascenus, 2. *orth. fid. c. 5.*).

15. And He did it in six distinct days, which is why creation is called by the fathers a *hexaemeron* work.

16. It seems agreeable to reason that all things were formed in a single moment, but this is contrary to the Mosaic Scripture.

17. On the first day, the heaven and the earth were created; that is, the raw and formless material of the entire work to come.

18. Light was also created to dispel the darkness of the abyss and to begin the cycle of days and nights.

19. That light was undoubtedly rather obscure. Therefore, the question concerning its nature is obscure.

20. On the second day, the firmament was made; that is, the entire system of heavenly bodies.

21. Above it, the Holy Spirit expressly states that there are waters; their purpose is known to Him who made them.

22. Let us believe the Scripture in this matter, whose authority is greater than the capacity of human ingenuity (Augustine, 2. *de Gen. ad lit. c. 4.*).

23. On the third day, the omnipotent rule of God gathers the sublunary waters and causes dry land to appear.

24. What, then, are the foundations of the earth? What are the boundaries of the sea? The omnipotent Word of God.

25. But God did not want the earth to be unfruitful; He commanded it to produce herbs of every kind (Isaiah 45:18).

---

[22] *in operibus ad extra agenda ordinem*

26. Those herbs are not all for man to eat, but they are all for man to use.

27. On the fourth day, God suspended the greater and lesser lights in the rafters of the firmament.

28. These are nothing other than the conveyors and vehicles of that original light.

29. The stars, both fixed and wandering, affect the things here below with their motion, light, and influence.

30. That influence is such that it is very obscure and not at all easy to determine.

31. Therefore, one must beware, lest we ascribe to the stars the causes for the wickedness of men, since the Creator of the stars is free from all wickedness.

32. "The wise will be governed by the stars." This should be understood concerning the true and divine wisdom which consists in the fear of God and in genuine godliness.

33. Therefore, it is not astrology, but vanity which strives to predict the fortunes, outcomes, and actions of men by means of the stars (Scal., *exerc.* 251.).

34. On the fifth day, the water is filled with fish, and the air with flying things.

35. From water God produces the things which are unable to live in the water and the things which only live in the water, which is an argument for His omnipotence and omnisapience.

36. The sixth day is the birthday of land animals and of man himself.

37. All these things were created for man, and man for God.

38. No creature would have harmed man; on the contrary, they would have all served him, if he had not sinned (Augustine, *lib.* 3. *de Gen. ad. lit. c.* 15.).

39. When man refused the service due to his Creator, he lost the dominion over the creatures that had been given to him.

40. As God was about to create man, He established a sort of foregone conclusion that man was to be created as a logical animal, capable of reason and counsel.

41. After all things were created, man is finally created, for he is the epitome, center, and complement of the whole universe.

42. He was also made on the earth and from the earth. Nevertheless, he was not made for the earth and for the sake of the earth, but for heaven and for the sake of heaven.

43. He who is the Creator of heaven and earth wanted to rest in man. Therefore, He rested after man was made.

44. Indeed, all things were made for man, so that God commanded the angels to serve man, although they are far superior in nature and in dignity.

45. And is it truly remarkable that all things were made by God for man, since God Himself was made man for man?

46. Moses does not describe the creation of the angels, but he does not remove them on that account from the list of created things.

47. On what day they were created is more logically asked than fruitfully discovered.

48. They are called 'spirits' due to their incorporeal nature, 'angels' due to their office.

49. They are spirits, but they do not rise to the simplicity of the divine nature.

50. Since the being and essence, acts and power, nature and actions in them are distinct.

51. They sometimes appear in bodies, but they are not corporeal, since the forms of their assumed bodies are attendant, not formative.

52. The angels understand through species both innate and added.

53. They call this knowledge of the angels 'evening' knowledge, to which they add 'morning' knowledge. They are said to know

all things intuitively by this light of the Word.

54. Oh, how easy it is for the intellect of little men, crawling around on the ground, to understand the intellect of the angels!

55. We do not fully know the mode of our own intelligence. And here we begin to babble about angelic intellect!

56. The angels are equipped, not only with intelligence, but also with power, for which reason they are called Powers and Authorities.

57. But this power of theirs is finite, just as their essence is also finite.

58. However, they are confined, not by the circumscription of a corporeal place, but by a designation of a definite 'where.'

59. Some say that the eternity of God is the measure of the angels (Scal., *ex. 359. sect. 7.*).

60. This should be understood of the measure of perfection, not of the measure of duration.

61. We do not deny that there are definite hierarchies among the angels, but we deny that it can be known to us what they are.

62. The ranks of angels are known to Him who ordained them.

63. We will see Him face to face, since we will one day be like the angels (Mat. 22:30).

64. All the angels were created by God good and perfect, for nothing but good and perfect can come from good and perfect.

65. But some of them—indeed, a large part—departed from that concreated goodness through a voluntary fall.

66. Who could relate the circumstances of the angels' fall, since the Scripture is silent? The fathers argue that it was pride or envy.

67. The evil angels fell without hope of restoration; but the good have been confirmed in goodness and have been freed from the danger of falling away.

68. This confirmation of the angels in goodness was not the equalized and due wages for some merit, but the free gift of the God who rewards beyond what is deserved.

69. From the confirmation of some angels in goodness and the hardening of others in evil arise the opposing works of each side.

70. The good angels are those who praise God and minister to men.

71. The angels are present with us to help us, to protect us, to fight for us (Bernard, *serm. 10. in Psa. 91.*).

72. The number of angels is innumerable to us.

73. Let those who have heard angels talking with one another discuss and determine how the angels talk with one another.

74. From their natural perceptiveness and the experience of the times, and even from higher revelation, the devils are able to know some things beforehand, but not all things.

75. They can do many wondrous things, but they are not properly called miracles.

76. They do what they can when God permits; they do not do what they can when God forbids.

77. This is the description of the first creative act of God in time, that is, of the kind of creation whose cause is the abundance and riches of divine goodness (Damascenus, *2. orth. fid. c. 2.*).

78. For it was not from neediness, but from beneficence that God made His works. He is not made greater by our praises, but is manifested by His works (*Euch., lib. 1. in Gen.*).

79. He is the final cause of the universe by reason of His kindness; the exemplary cause, by reason of His wisdom; the efficient cause, by reason of His power (Thomas, *1. q. 46. art. 1.*).

80. Therefore, the glory of God is the ultimate goal of the creation; the use of men is the secondary and intermediate goal.

81. The good God did all things well and made all things good. To Him be praise, honor, and glory forever and ever.

Chapter 6: Providence

1. God is not only the almighty Creator, but also the almighty Sustainer and Governor of the universe.

2. He did all things well; He governs and administers all things well.

3. Just as nothing was made apart from His creative essence, so nothing thrives apart from the preserving power of the same (Anselm, *in Monol.*).

4. This divine sustenance and governance of all created things is usually called Providence.

5. Nature itself bears clear witness to this; but Holy Scripture bears even clearer witness.

6. The laws of true piety declare that all things exist and are governed by divine providence (Eusebius, 6. *de praepar. Evang. cap.* 5.).

7. Now providence consists in these three things: foreknowledge, purpose, and administration.

8. Hugo de S. Victor expresses it in this way: In providence, one must consider the guiding knowledge, the ruling will, and the implementing power.

9. Foreknowledge is the very present view of all things, past, present, and future.

10. God views absolutely all things in the now, not wavering, but fixed, not advancing, but steady and immovable.

11. He excludes all spaces and intervals of time from the character of His eternity.

12. As He does not remember the past from a distance, so He also does not foresee the future, but sees all things in the present.

13. The mutable things are known; they transpire and advance. But the vision of the Knowing One ignores the turns of change (Polycratic., *lib. 2. cap. 21.*).

14. By this knowledge, all things are more familiar to God than they are to themselves.

15. God sees Himself in Himself; He sees everything else in Himself, for from Him and in Him are all things.

16. This knowledge of God is immutable; nonetheless, the things to which His knowledge extends are, in themselves, mutable.

17. All things are necessary by necessity of the consequence, but not by necessity of the consequent.

18. For it cannot be unknown to the omniscient God how the force of acting will change direction in the causes that are contingently and freely acting.

19. Meanwhile, by that vision of His, He does not introduce any absolute necessity into them, or else they would cease to be free and contingent acts.

20. Therefore, it is disgraceful to ascribe to divine providence the necessity of perpetrating disgraceful things.

21. If man sinned because God foreknew that he would sin, then God foreknew not the sins of man but His own sins, which is wickedness.

22. God foresees, not only the 'what,' but also the 'through which' and the 'how,' the cause and the manner of acting.

23. He foresees the things; He foresees the cause of the things. Therefore, the things that are voluntary or contingent from their own causes do not cease to be such through divine providence.

24. How can the order of causes, which is certain to the foreknowing God, bring about the result that nothing is in our will, when our decisions take place within that very order of causes?

25. But providence is not bare foreknowledge, since God is not a leisurely spectator of things; it is also predestination or pur-

pose, the will and decree that provides for all things ahead of time.

26. To foresee is not only to have knowledge, but also the benevolent will to provide.

27. That eternal purpose looks precisely to the actual administration of things in time.

28. For whatever God does and however He acts in time by His administration, that He also decreed from eternity to do and to act in that way by His purpose.

29. Administration is the actual and temporal sustaining and governing of all things by which God wisely, freely, powerfully, and beneficially guides and controls all things.

30. This administration extends to absolutely all things; it reaches mightily from one end to the other and sweetly orders all things (Wisdom 8:1).

31. For if it is not an injury and disgrace to God to have made each tiny thing, much less is it a disgrace to Him to rule over the things that have been made (Ambrose, *1. de offic. cap. 13.*).

32. Since all things were made from nothing, all things would return to nothing if that supreme and true Being did not sustain all things. This preservation is nothing other than the continuation of existence (Scal. *exerc. 250. sect. 1.*).

33. As the existence of sunbeams depends on the sun, as the existence of a shadow depends on a body, so the existence of all creatures depends on divine preservation (Raym. de Sabaud., *in Theol. natur. cap. 16.*).

34. Not only does God preserve the created things, but He also governs, guides, and directs them.

35. But while all things have been subjected to divine governance, God is particularly concerned with the human race, and especially with the Church gathered from the human race.

36. By this providence of His, God ordinarily preserves the course of nature that has been instituted.

37. For He administers things in such a way that He permits them to exercise their own movements (Augustine, 7. de Civ. Dei cap. 30.).

38. Divine providence ordinarily acts through means; but our trust does not lie in the means.

39. For there is no efficacy of the secondary causes that does not descend from the primary cause.

40. Moreover, providence is not bound to the means in such a way that it cannot carry out its works without them.

41. The power of all the secondary causes rests eminently and causally in the first.

42. Therefore, a defect in the secondary causes can easily be supplied by the power of the first.

43. Although the secondary causes have been set in motion, nevertheless, divine providence can change and impede their effect.

44. Since the secondary causes cannot act apart from the influence of the first.

45. Indeed, divine providence knows how to use the secondary causes to produce an effect that differs from what their character allows.

46. He who gave the laws and order of nature is not bound to the laws and order of nature.

47. The animals themselves, with a certain natural instinct, sense this providence by which they are sustained and directed.

48. The ingress, progress, and egress of human life is of particular concern to God.

49. He is said to form in the womb (Job 10:8), to draw forth from the womb (Psa. 22:10).

50. He rules our life in such a way that even the falling hairs of our head do not fall apart from His will (Mat. 10:30).

51. He establishes a boundary for man which he is unable to pass (Job 14:5).

52. Nevertheless, divine providence guides the course and outcome of human life in such a way that it neither excludes secondary causes nor is bound to them.

53. From this, you will understand that marriages are of fate in such a way that they are, nevertheless, sometimes fatuous.

54. And that the end of life is, indeed, certain, but it is not determined by some law and Stoic necessity of the Fates.

55. As divine providence guides the life of men, so, too, does He guide their actions.

56. But sometimes He accompanies good actions, sometimes evil.

57. He guides civilly good actions in such a way that He not only preserves the acting nature and grants the power to act, but also approves and aids those actions and, in a peculiar way, sometimes drives men to them.

58. He commands and approves spiritually good actions in such a way that He effects them through His Spirit in us and through us.

59. But He neither commands, nor desires, nor aids evil actions, nor drives men to them.

60. For one must seek not so much the efficient cause, but the deficient cause of evil (Augustine, *12. de Civ. Dei cap. 7.*).

61. For evil is not a work of God, but something that is lacking from His work (Augustine, *14. de Civ. Dei cap. 11.*).

62. The most perfect and pure God cannot be lacking from His acts; therefore, He cannot be the cause of evil.

63. Divine providence concurs in evil actions by foreknowing, by upholding nature, by permitting, by forsaking, by handing over to Satan, by setting boundaries ahead of time, and by eliciting good from them.

64. He hardens *negatively* by not softening, *privatively* by withdrawing all softness, *paradotically* by handing man over to him-

self and to Satan to be hardened, *materially* by showing signs and wonders, and *constitutively* by directing the hardness to a good end.

65. Thus Suidas shows from the fathers that God administers all things according to a certain order: according to His good pleasure in good things, according to His permission in evil things.

66. That permission is not the permission of one who is imprudent, nor of one who is simply unwilling, nor of one who is worried, nor of one who is an idle spectator, nor of one who gives free rein to the undertakings of men and of Satan; no, it is the permission of the entirely just Avenger and of the perfectly wise Governor.

67. God punishes sins with sins in such a way that He is still not the cause of sins.

68. And since divine providence does not exclude secondary causes, nor does He normally change their character, for this reason, certain things, due to a particular cause, can be called 'chance' and 'fortuitous' which, nevertheless, do not escape the order of the universal cause.

69. Chance and fortune are expressions of human ignorance (Augustine, *5. de Civit. Dei cap. 9.*).

70. Pious meditation on divine providence will be able to have this effect in us, that we are neither elated in prosperity nor despairing in adversity.

71. Let us commit our whole selves and all that we have to Him who cares for each one of us as He would care for only one, who cares for all just as He would care for each.

Chapter 7: Election and Reprobation

1. Predestination is a peculiar action of divine providence which is concerned with the salvation of men.

2. For through it, the rational creature is directed toward a goal which exceeds his proportion, namely, eternal life.

3. In this sense, predestination is established as a part of divine providence (Thomas, *p. 1. q. 23. art. 1.*).

4. The doctrine of predestination should not be concealed in a cloud of silence, since it is revealed in the Scriptures by the Holy Spirit.

5. But it should be treated soberly, reverently, and prudently.

6. Let us say, not what and as much as the curiosity of the human heart desires, but what and as much as the mastery of the Holy Spirit supplies.

7. That which God has revealed for our edification should not be converted into some men's destruction.

8. Predestination, as to the term, is not only the preceding determination of the goal, but also of the means that lead to the goal.

9. Predestination and election march in lockstep with one another in the Scriptures.

10. Therefore, we know of no predestination to eternal death.

11. Otherwise, it would follow that God also predestined the causes of eternal death, namely, unbelief and sins, which would be wicked.

12. For God did not predestine the wicked to lose righteousness as He predestined the saints to receive it (Fulg., *lib. 1. ad Mon.*).

13. Otherwise, it would follow that God predestined some men to the former, even though He Himself arranged to forbid the same with a commandment, and to temper it with mercy, and to punish it with justice.

14. Predestination or election is also referred to as a writing into the Book of Life.

15. For that Book of Life does not remind God of some men, lest He forget about them; it signifies the predestination of those to whom eternal life will be given (Augustine, 20. *de Civ. Dei c. 15.*).

16. Therefore, just as none of the elect shall perish, so those who are written in the Book of Life will never be erased from it.

17. Moreover, speaking properly and according to the language of Scripture, the ones who are said to be written in the Book of Life are those who cling to Christ with persevering faith.

18. Election is, no less than creation, an immediate act of the one and only God.

19. It views the Son of God, not only as He is one God with the Father and the Holy Spirit, but also as He is the appointed Mediator.

20. In this sense, we are not only said to be elected by Christ, but also in Christ (Eph. 1:4).

21. It is, moreover, not an emanant, but an immanent act.

22. The act was ordained, and thus the elect are said to have been ordained to eternal life (Acts 13:48).

23. The Gospel manifests to us the rationale of that ordination; through the Gospel, the mystery of our eternal salvation, which was hidden in eternal times, is revealed in time (Rom. 16:26).

24. In this sense, election is said to have been done according to the purpose and foreknowledge of God (Eph. 1:11; 1 Pet. 1:2).

25. That purpose is the counsel and good pleasure of God concerning the salvation of men through faith in Christ.

26. Likewise, foreknowledge must necessarily be related to

a consideration of faith[23], for God did not elect to eternal life all those whom He foreknew in any way; He elected those whom He foresaw would steadfastly believe in Christ by the grace of the Holy Spirit.

27. He elected, moreover, by grace, not according to the foreseen merits of works.

28. The cause and the sole foundation of that grace is Christ. We have been freely loved in the Beloved (Eph. 1:6).

29. But since Christ is of no benefit to anyone apart from faith, the mention of Christ in this matter includes the concept of faith.

30. In this sense, we are not only said to be elected in Christ, but also in faith (2 The. 2:13).

31. In turn, since eternal life is the goal, not of a fleeting faith, but of one that steadfastly perseveres, therefore perseverance in faith is implied.

32. With respect to us, the goal of election is sanctification in the kingdom of grace and glorification in the kingdom of glory.

33. With respect to God, the goal of election is His own glory and the visible manifestation of His mercy.

34. Therefore, they absolutely go astray who invent an absolute decree of election.

35. If the decree of election were absolute, then the decree of reprobation would also be absolute, since the reason of the contraries is the same[24].

36. But the beneficent will of God, which genuinely seeks the salvation of all men, is opposed to an absolute decree of reprobation.

37. This is attested by the words of Scripture, by the tears of Christ, and by the oath of God Himself.

38. Nothing absolute should be imagined here. God wills—genuinely wills!—the life of the sinner. But He also wills the sinner's conversion through the Word and the Holy Spirit.

---

23   *ad fidei intuitum*
24   *cum contrariorum eadem sit ratio*

39. If a sinner spurns that Word and resists the Holy Spirit, and thus is not converted, God wills the just condemnation of the sinner.

40. These things are not opposed to each other, but demonstrate the wondrous balance of divine justice and mercy.

41. The things concerning the hidden will of God, which some suggest are contrary to the will revealed in the Word, since they have not been revealed, are rightly hidden from the godly.

42. Nor does God testify with words alone that He genuinely seeks the salvation of all, but also by the matter itself.

43. In the first Adam, He formed all for eternal life (in a seminal manner); in the second Adam, He restored all to eternal life.

44. The first Adam was created in the image of God, of which immortality was a part.

45. All men were in the loins of that first parent. Therefore, one can say that they were all formed in the image of God and for immortality.

46. This investiture of life which happened to all in our first parent is clearly at odds with the absolute predestination of some to death.

47. He who denies that a universal restoration was made through Christ denies the truth written in the Word by the rays of the sun.

48. Christ is said to have died, not only indefinitely for men, but also universally for all, and even specifically and notably for those who perish.

49. They do not belong to the shores of the world who take such expressions to be about the better part of the world.

50. For the obedience of the second Adam was not of lesser worth than the guilt incurred by the disobedience of the first.

51. They assert their bare fancies apart from Scripture who argue that Christ only seemed to have died for those who perish.

52. They do not answer sufficiently who claim that Christ died for all only sufficiently, but not efficiently.

53. Because they ascribe the cause of that inefficacy to an absolute decree of God, not only to the fault of men.

54. That which Christ acquired for all by His precious blood is offered to all by the Holy Spirit in the precious deposit of the Word.

55. The Gospel is offered to all; in the Gospel, the benefits of Christ; in the benefits of Christ, the grace of God; in the grace of God, eternal life.

56. And thus the Father's love, the Son's satisfaction, and the Holy Spirit's call are always connected.

57. That call, in and of itself, with respect to the God who calls, is universal, for He commands that the Gospel be proclaimed to all.

58. But it is rendered particular by the fault of men, who deprive both themselves and their posterity of such a great treasure by their contempt for the Word.

59. In this sense, they are said to judge themselves unworthy of eternal life (Acts 13:46).

60. If it is traced down to the smallest details, we admit that many things are still obscure in the light of grace that will one day be clear to all in the light of glory.

61. The grace of the God who calls differs according to persons and times, but it is denied to no one by absolute decree (Prosper., *1. de vocat. gent. cap. 5.*).

62. Neither should the grace of God, who calls all men, be humbled, nor should the powers of free will, which receives His grace, be exalted.

63. Let the salvation of men be acknowledged as the gift of divine grace alone; let the condemnation of men be understood as the merit of human guilt alone.

64. Let the judgments of God always be acknowledged as just, even though they are not always clear to us.

65. Divine grace comes first and prepares us before we are able; it operates in us so that we are able; it cooperates with us once we are enabled by its own gift.

66. From all these things, it is clear that neither the decree of election nor that of reprobation is absolute.

67. God did not only execute the decree of election through Christ, but He also made the decree of election in Christ.

68. For just as God justifies and saves men in time, in the same way He also decreed from eternity to justify and save them.

69. The act of God in time is a mirror of the decree concerning that act made without time.

70. The cause of this is the immutability of the divine will.

71. Consequently, just as God saves all and only those who persevere in believing in Christ in time, so He also determined from eternity to save all and only those who would persevere in believing in Christ. That is, He elected them to eternal life.

72. Therefore, the sober teaching and meditation on predestination begins with the wounds of Christ.

73. The true light of Christ shines on us in the light of the Word. In Christ shines the heart of God, who elects us to salvation.

74. Apart from the light and path of the Word, anything that is either devised here by the mind or uttered by the lips is mist, is error.

75. On the other hand, by following the light of the Word, we shall stray neither to the right of presumptuous temerity, nor to the left of carnal security.

Chapter 8: The Image of God in Man after the Fall

1. The creation of man in God's image in time followed the decree of predestination made outside of time.

2. If only the image of God in the first man were as clearly known to us as it once prevailed for affording the highest grace to our race!

3. But the full recognition of it escapes our intellect, even as the possession of it sadly perished long ago.

4. We can only speak of it in a way similar to those who are incarcerated in dark dungeons, who investigate the excellence of a light which is unknown to them.

5. The apostle explains that the image of God has to do with righteousness and holiness of truth (Eph. 4:24).

6. Since these are in a list of qualities and virtues, it is clear that the image refers more to a likeness in virtues than to nature.

7. The same nature has essentially remained in man after the Fall that was in him prior to the Fall.

8. But since we are now said to be renewed in the image of God, therefore the image of God is not the essence itself of the rational soul, for clearly this also exists in those who are not born again.

9. That which is finally to be obtained through renewal is not produced through the old flesh.

10. The gift which is obtained through regeneration is not possessed through carnal generation.

11. The image of God is restored in the reborn through a renewal in knowledge (Col. 3:10).

12. The light of divine knowledge is not a concreated attribute of the human soul after the Fall, but a conformity of the reborn

with God that is engendered from the gift and illumination of the Holy Spirit.

13. From this it follows that the image of God is not to be defined by those things which apply essentially to the soul of the man who has not also been reborn.

14. That primeval righteousness and holiness in which the apostle established the image of God embraces the light of divine knowledge and wisdom in the mind, the complete conformity with God's Law in the will, and the uprightness of all the soul's powers and affections in the heart.

15. Man was a living mirror of wisdom, kindness, charity, righteousness, holiness, and divine purity.

16. Reason was perfectly subject to God; to reason was subject the will; to the will were subject the emotions and the remaining powers.

17. There was no servile fear in man, no sadness; there was a blessed peace and a perpetual exultation in the Creator-God.

18. Therefore, man did not only know God externally from His creation, but he also had the living letters of divine knowledge internally within himself.

19. Man bore the image of God as a son bears the image of his father, to whom he owes devotion and love; as a servant bears the image of his lord, to whom he owes reverence and fear; as a soldier bears the image of his general, to whom he owes obedience and loyalty; as a steward bears the image of his master, to whom he owes an exact accounting of his administration.

20. The nakedness of man was an external symbol of his inner innocence and cleanness; his dwelling in Paradise showed his inner tranquility and happiness.

21. There was no movement in the body to which shame might be owed. Man thought to cover nothing, for he felt nothing that needed to be restrained (Aug., *11 de Gen. ad lit. c. 1.*).

22. To attribute to the first man a certain wrestling between the higher and lower powers of the soul wrestles against the perfection of the first man.

23. Nor do they teach soundly who claim that some feebleness was healed and repressed in the first man by the antidote of original righteousness.

24. They are worthy of hatred who argue that evil desires worthy of God's hatred immediately arose from a material condition in the first man, considered in a purely natural state.

25. It is an insult to God, the Author of nature, to assert that evil desires arise in a man from a material condition which is evil in and of itself.

26. Nor do the wisdom and power of God permit us to say that such evil desires arose from a material condition aside from His intention.

27. For who will suffer to hear that this is attributed to the works of God: a flagon begins to be crafted on the pottery wheel, and soon a pot emerges?

28. What could have arisen beyond His intention, apart from whose intention nothing arises?

29. If, to any extent, the remnants of that divine image still remaining after the Fall are natural to man, then there was certainly also a primeval uprightness that was natural to the first man.

30. For in creatures of the same kind, attributes are rightly passed on from the nature of the part to the nature of the whole.

31. The image of God would have been propagated to later men through natural generation. But now the things that are propagated naturally are the very things that are also natural.

32. From all these things it is clear that the image of God was not some external and supernatural adornment in the first man, like a virgin's wreath or Samson's strength; but a certain intrinsic and concreated virtue.

33. Nevertheless, it was not the very substance of man, nor was it some essential part of man.

34. Man is said to have been created in the image of God. Therefore, man himself was one thing, the image of God in him was another.

35. Holiness and righteousness are essentially proper to God alone, while they are only inherently proper to man.

36. A certain part of His divine image was immortality, for God made man to be immortal (Wisdom 2:23).

37. The death of the body, to which we were all subjected after the Fall, is not some sort of natural condition of man, but a penalty that passes down from the offense of the transgression.

38. It is not the debt of the nature established by God, but the merit of man who departs from God.

39. How could man, existing as a mortal, have copied the image of the immortal God in himself?

40. When man opened the door of sin to Satan, who was knocking, then death entered for him and all his descendants (Rom. 5:12).

41. That immortality for which the first man was created, as well as the whole image of God itself, was a sort of natural and intrinsic characteristic of the human nature.

42. There was a perfect harmony of all the qualities in the body, and he was ruled by the soul which was created in the image and immortality of God.

43. Therefore, even as we, after the Fall, are, by nature, children of wrath and of death (Eph. 2:3), so the first man, before the Fall, was, by nature, a child of grace and of life.

44. Nevertheless, one degree of immortality was established in nature, another will one day be fully restored in nature.

45. The immortality of the first man consisted in being able not to die; the immortality of the elect will finally consist in not being able to die (Augustine, 6. *de Gen. ad lit. cap.* 25.).

46. And since immortality was a part of the divine image, it is clear that the image of God also shone forth in a certain way in the body of man.

47. The beauty of the vestment also revealed the handsomeness of the spirit (Bernard, *Serm. 24. super Cant. col. 564.*).

48. To the one who asks whether Eve was also created in the image of God, we reply that the word 'image' is among those things which are declared to be 'from one thing to another.'[25]

49. Firstly and principally, the image of God shone forth in the conformity of man's soul and of all his powers with the Law of God, which was common to both sexes, though in different degrees.

50. Secondly, the image of God shone in that external privilege of dominion, of which the preeminence properly belonged to the man.

51. Nor did man lack anything he needed for happiness, besides the grace of body and soul, and also the grace of the place God had given him as a habitation, namely, Paradise.

52. Man was created by God as spiritual and physical. Therefore he had a twofold Paradise, both spiritual and physical.

53. The physical or earthly Paradise was a likeness and a training ground of the heavenly Paradise, which is inward and spiritual, that is, the highest tranquility and happiness in the mind of man.

54. In what geographical region of the earth the physical Paradise was located, we will show to him who plainly shows us what the geography of the earth was like before the Flood.

55. If anyone claims that the Garden of Eden still survives, we will believe him, as long as he brings us a branch from it or demonstrates, with suitably sound arguments, that it survives.

56. Indeed, Enoch and Elijah live, not in that earthly Paradise, but in the heavenly one which Christ promised to the thief (Luke 23:43).

---

25   ἀφ' ἑνὸς πρὸς ἕν

57. Two special trees made the garden of Paradise famous: the tree of life and the tree of knowledge (Gen. 2:9).

58. There was on display in the tree of life a preventative medicine for man against sickness and old age, as also a Sacrament of eternal blessedness.

59. The tree of knowledge was man's altar and temple. By abstaining from its fruit, due obedience was to be offered to the Creator.

60. This tree was so named from what happened after the fall. By picking its fruit, man learns by experience how much good he has lost through sin, and how much evil he has brought on himself by his own disobedience.

61. On the basis of the propagation of the divine image from the first man to his descendants, which would have endured if he himself had endured, we also conclude that souls were propagated.

62. For since the image of God cannot exist in the human body outside of and apart from the soul, it is also necessary that the soul itself should be propagated to the one who has been propagated.

63. The propagation of original sin, which has passed down in place of the divine image, proves that this propagation of souls still endures.

64. Therefore, as from the animated rib of Adam, the animated woman was once formed, so from the animated parents, the animated children today are propagated.

65. We will defend the opinion of those who claim the daily and immediate creation of souls, if they will show us definitively how souls do not come from Adam, while still coming under the just sentence of damnation from him (Augustine, *Epist. 157.*).

66. We affirm the propagation of souls; we leave the manner of propagation for others to investigate and debate.

67. God is said to give souls, for the activity of all natural causes is from Him (Scal., *ex. 188. sect. 1.*).

68. But it is too much to infer that, since He is said to form the body in the womb, He also gives souls by immediate creation.

69. We do not disapprove of the restraint of those who say that it is sufficient for their faith to know where they are going, by living piously, even if they do not know from whence they came (Augustine, *10. de Gen. ad lit. c. 23.*).

70. Let the origin of the soul lie hidden, as long as the propagation of original sin and the redemption of souls remains clear (Aug., *Epist. 157. ad Optat.*).

71. The Holy Spirit proves, and experience convinces us, that the image of God, if it is understood according to the language of Scripture as true righteousness and holiness, has been lost.

72. For what else is the sin of origin but the lack of the divine image which has passed down in place of that primeval integrity?

73. Nevertheless, this image has been lost in such a way that slight remnants of it survive, which are like the ruins and shadow of a great name.

74. This doctrine of the image of God leads us to the knowledge of divine kindness and of our misery, and it supports the expectation of our hope.

75. Praise be to God the Father, who, in Adam, made us in His image. Praise be to the Son, who again earned for us the renewal of that image. Praise be to the Holy Spirit, through whom that image, in turn, begins to be renewed in us.

Chapter 9: Original Sin

That is, the fall of our first parents and the consequent corruption of nature that has been propagated into their descendants.

1. The first man did not persevere in his concreated integrity and perfection. Therefore, it did not pass down to his descendants by hereditary right.

2. He followed the deceitful persuasion of the serpent, and thus he fell into the wicked transgression of the divine commandment.

3. In that natural serpent lay hidden the infernal serpent.

4. Therefore, the serpent was filled and resonated with the voice of the devil, who seduced the first men with his craftiness.

5. He approached the woman, who was not entirely equal to the man in powers of discernment.

6. By deceitfully questioning her about the meaning of the commandment, he incites her to perilous doubt.

7. He questions her externally with a counterfeit voice; he wounds her spirit internally with poisonous fangs; and he breathes into her the venom of doubt.

8. Afterward, made even bolder by his success, he turns Eve's doubt into open denial.

9. He, the most malevolent, accuses God of malevolence. He, the most removed from divine wisdom, deceives with a lying promise of divine preeminence and wisdom.

10. Therefore, the causes of the primeval fall are the devil, who tempts, and the man, who freely consents.

11. God, as the One who is good and the Author of nothing but good, should by no means be connected to this fall.

12. As God created man in the beginning, so He wanted him ever to remain, nor did He force man to fall by some hidden decree or control.

13. God is not the Author of that of which He is the vindicator and avenger; the iniquity which He punishes, He Himself did not commit (Fulgent., *lib. 1. ad Monim.*).

14. Before man fell, God had given him the perfect resources so that he was able not to fall, an uninjured will so that he was able not to want to fall; He had added the most severe threat of death so that he might not fall.

15. Man was not made to want to sin. And while he was formed with the freedom to be able to want to sin, he was also adorned with such great light that he was able not to want to sin.

16. You say in vain that, if man had not sinned, then God would not have had occasion to exercise mercy and righteousness.

17. For God does not need the righteousness of the upright; how much less does He need the iniquity of the perverse! (Augustine, *11. de Genes. ad lit. cap. 7.*)

18. Nor is God perfected by external works, which are only the traces and evidences of internal perfection.

19. The sequence of the Mosaic description shows that unbelief was man's first sin.

20. As long as the Word and faith are retained in the heart, a person does not show disdain toward God.

21. And whatever the sequence of internal intentions was, unbelief was the first sin in the external act of commission.

22. Nor would the mind of man, illuminated by divine light, have turned itself away from God through exaltation, unless it had previously departed from the Word.

23. The apostle denies that Adam was seduced (1 Tim.

2:14), which should be understood concerning the manner and order of seduction.

24. Even if Adam was not seduced by another, nevertheless, he was seduced by himself.

25. People ask in vain whether Adam's sin or Eve's was the more serious. They sinned differently with regard to their gender, but equally with regard to their contempt.

26. The opening of their eyes after the fall is nothing other than the sense of sin and the prick of a trembling conscience.

27. They saw that they were naked; that is, that they had been stripped of the clothing of concreated integrity and innocence. Their nakedness was not unknown to them before the fall, but it was not shameful or indecent.

28. They saw that their flesh was incited with pricks of lust, and that the law of their members struggled shamefully against the law of their mind.

29. Just how much darkness seized their mind through the fall is readily apparent from the fact that they thought they could hide in the shade of the trees from Him whose eyes are brighter than the sun.

30. They wanted to hide from Him from whom nothing can hide, and to cover their flesh from Him who is the inspector of the heart (Augustine, *11. de Genes. ad lit. c. 34.*).

31. To the blindness of the mind was joined the trembling of the heart. They who formerly rejoiced in the conversation and the sight of God were frightened by the sound of a leaf.

32. They are called to the tribunal of God, before the One who pleads on their behalf, and thus their Ally becomes their Prosecutor.

33. This sin of our first parents corrupted and putrefied the human nature that was wholly within them and of which there was nothing outside of them (Anselm, *de conc. virg. cap. 2.*).

34. Adam was, and in him we all were. Adam perished, and we all perish in him (Ambrose, in *cap. 15. Lucae.*).

35. Because the parents lost the feud, the children are considered to have lost it.

36. From a corrupt root spring forth bad fruits; from an unclean fountain flow dirty rivers; from leprous parents are born leprous children.

37. Thus from the first parents, devoid of original righteousness and infected with the stain of sin, are born children of the same kind, devoid of righteousness, infected with sin.

38. For Adam did not beget a son in the image of God, but in his own image, corrupted by sin (Gen. 5:3).

39. The personal sin of Adam corrupts the nature; the corruption of the nature is propagated by carnal generation into the person of the offspring.

40. Adam sinned, not as a private man, but as the mass and head of the human race.

41. As the nature is propagated to his descendants, so also the corruption of his nature; as sin is propagated, so also the guilt which results from sin.

42. Indeed, this is what original sin is said to be. Those who either deny or diminish it detract not a little from the grace of God.

43. The preachers of nature are enemies of grace.

44. Not only do the manifest oracles of the Holy Spirit testify to this original sin, but all actual sins also testify to it, as do the heavy burdens of manifold calamities and death, and finally, the regeneration to eternal life, which is necessary for everyone.

45. Therefore, vain and frivolous is that assertion of Pelagius that sin entered into the world by imitation, not by propagation.

46. Indeed, death—the wages of sin—also reigns in those who did not sin in the likeness of Adam's transgression (Rom. 5:14).

47. The apostle pronounces us children of wrath, not by imitation, but by nature (Eph. 2:3).

48. This sin is called 'original,' not from the origin of either the universal or human nature, but from the origin of each person born of Adam after the fall.

49. Indeed, it is also called 'original,' because of the actual sins of which it is the common fount and origin.

50. As to what original sin is, it is not only the lack of original righteousness, but also the imposition of a wicked quality. The result of both is guilt.

51. From this our parents cause us to be damned even before we are born (Bernard. *in Medit. cap. 2. col. 1190.*).

52. The depraved concupiscence in which the power of this evil especially manifests itself is not only the penalty and cause of sin, but is itself sin.

53. For to it belongs the disobedience against the rule of the mind (Augustine, *lib. 5. contra Julian. cap. 3.*).

54. The vice of concupiscence exists, not only in the lower faculties of the soul, but also in the higher ones.

55. Indeed, the will of the man who is not yet regenerated is prone to evil and vanities.

56. Among the works of the flesh are included heresies, idolatry, enmity, etc. (Gal. 5:20).

57. From this, it is clearly gathered that 'the flesh' is understood to be the whole man, as he is after the fall, apart from the grace of God and regeneration.

58. Through the sin of origin, the whole nature of man is thoroughly and intimately corrupt, but the vice must be distinguished from the very substance of man, which is a benefit of God and of nature.

59. Men are conceived in sin. Therefore, they are not sin itself.

60. The subject of original sin is the whole man, with all the powers of the soul and with all the members of the body.

61. Original righteousness was not only the steady temperament of the body, but also the uprightness and inner adornment of all the powers of the soul.

62. Thus the original sin which took its place is not some diseased quality of the body, but the infection of all the powers of the soul.

63. For the behavior and the privations revolve around the same subject.

64. This evil is propagated through carnal generation.

65. For this reason, man after the fall is flesh, because he is born of flesh (John 3:3). He is by nature a child of wrath (Eph. 2:3). Therefore, he contracts sin by being born, for which reason he is a child of wrath.

66. Therefore, as many as are born of parents by carnal generation are born subject to original sin.

67. Consequently, also the children of reborn believers carry this original scourge with them into the world.

68. For it is not generation, but regeneration that produces Christians (Augustine, 3. *de peccat. merit. et remiss. cap. 9.*).

69. Christians are made, not born (Tertullian, *in Apolog. cap. 17.*).

70. Only He was born without sin who was conceived in the virgin's womb by the Holy Spirit, without a man's seed.

71. He is not infected with the blemish of sin who was born holy, of sanctified entrails.

72. Indeed, we do not even admit the blessed virgin into the possession of this dignity.

73. We say that Mary conceived gloriously of the Holy Spirit, not that she was also thus conceived. We say that the virgin gave birth, not that she was also given birth by a virgin (Bernard, *Epist. 174. ad Lugdun.*).

74. Some effects of original sin are penalties only, others are penalties and sins.

75. The penalties are both temporal and eternal, inasmuch as the misfortunes are manifold: innumerable streams of diseases, temporal death, the wrath of God, [and] eternal damnation.

76. The depraved motivations of concupiscence, the damnable feelings of the heart, and the finishing touch of actual sins are at once the sins and the penalties.

77. The guilt of original sin always drags us on to commit sins. (Cassiodorus, *in Psa. 118.*)

78. The number of those actual sins is truly innumerable to us, for who understands his faults? (Psa. 19:13.)

79. The blood of Jesus Christ cleanses believers from all sins, both original and actual (1 John 1:8).

80. For we were sprinkled with His blood in Baptism, which is for that very reason a holy and salutary washing of regeneration (Titus 3:5).

81. To this regeneration, renewal is joined with an indivisible bond. Such renewal is not entirely complete in this life.

82. For if perfect renewal occurred in Baptism, the apostle would not say that the inner man is being renewed day by day (Augustine, *2. de peccat. merit. & remiss. cap. 7.*).

83. Therefore, having recognized the extreme corruption of our nature, let us sigh with longing for Christ, the Physician, and for the perfect renewal that awaits in eternal life.

Chapter 10: Free Will

That is, the human powers that still remain after the fall.

1. The poison of original sin has thoroughly invaded and intimately corrupted all the powers of man.
2. For this reason they have suffered a tremendous decrease and reduction.
3. The powers of man should be considered especially from the rational soul made in the image of God.
4. There are two faculties of the rational soul: the mind that understands and the will that chooses.
5. From the confluence of both powers is born that which is commonly called 'free will,' an act of deliberate choice[26].
6. Free will is a faculty of the mind and the will, for the will is of the mind, and the freedom is of the will.
7. Freedom is attributed to the will, first, with respect to the mode of acting, which is free and voluntary.
8. For the will is neither coerced nor forcefully seized by external motivation, nor does it act solely by natural instinct, but has an internal and free starting point of its own motivation.
9. This freedom is a natural and essential property of the will.
10. It was not lost, therefore, through the fall.
11. For the will did not cease to be the will through the fall.
12. It is said to be the freedom from coercion, from necessity; a freedom that is internal and in the subject.
13. Consequently, the will of man is always free in this respect, although not always good (Augustine, *in Enchir. cap. 30.*).

---

26   προαίρεσις

14. Yet the will of man is free in such a way that it is forced to acknowledge the rule of God.

15. And thus it is not free from duty and obligation.

16. For God has impressed on the human mind the natural knowledge, whose light and leading the will ought to follow.

17. If it follows such knowledge, it is truly free.

18. For it is truly freedom to serve God and righteousness.

19. In this sense, Tullius is not wrong when he says: We are slaves of laws so that we can be free (*pro Cluent.*).

20. Therefore, with respect to freedom from coercion, man always has a free will, even after the fall.

21. But with respect to freedom from obligation, man never has a free will, not even before the fall.

22. The freedom of the will is also considered with respect to its object, which is good or evil.

23. This is called freedom toward an object and inner freedom.

24. From a consideration of the diverse states of man it becomes known what that freedom of human will is like.

25. The freedom of will in man before the fall was a faculty of reason and will by which man was able to sin and to not sin, to stand and to fall (Anselm, *De lib. arbitr. cap. 7.*).

26. For his will was not yet immutably limited to good.

27. The will of man was established to go in one of two ways; life and death were set before him (Ecc. 15:18).

28. The light of wisdom shone in his mind; in his will there was a conformity with God as the Archtype. Meanwhile, he was left with the freedom either to persevere in concreated goodness or to fall away from it.

29. This can be called a freedom of uprightness, a freedom from slavery and misery.

30. Nor was it an essential property of the will, but a separable accident.

31. Accordingly, it could be lost through the fall, and, tragically, it was indeed lost.

32. By using his free will poorly, man destroys both it and himself (Augustine, *in Enchir. cap. 30.*).

33. In this respect, the will of man is no longer free, but captive and enslaved.

34. In committing sin, he has become a slave of sin (John 8:34).

35. Since the image of God was lost through the fall, the freedom of uprightness and the ability to choose good were lost at the same time.

36. In its place, there followed an extreme corruption of powers, and an unbridled impetus to do evil.

37. For this reason, the will of man is only free to do evil after the fall, which is a wretched and miserable freedom.

38. Indeed, it should rather be considered a most sorrowful slavery.

39. The apostle calls it a freedom from righteousness, for in refusing to serve righteousness, man became subject to the yoke of the evil mistress iniquity. (Rom. 6:20, Augustine, *de verb. Apost. serm. 12.*)

40. The soul of man, under this voluntary and wretchedly free necessity, is held to be both maidservant and free.

41. Maidservant on account of necessity, free on account of will (Bernard, *serm. 81. sup. Cant.*).

42. The will of man after the fall is prone to evil, and yet it does not cease to be free, because it is not forced to do evil, but willingly chooses it.

43. From this, it is clear that the inner freedom of the will is able to coexist with the slavery of sin…

44. In the same way that freedom coexists with the immutability of doing good and confirmation in goodness.

45. The first of these applies to God, the second to the good angels.

46. Therefore, there remained a free will in man, even after the fall, if it is understood as a freedom from coercion.

47. Free will perished in man, if it is understood as the power to choose good and to avoid evil.

48. Accordingly, the concreated light which shone in the mind of the first man was replaced with darkness (Eph. 5:8).

49. Consequently, the intellect of man was not only blinded in the salutary and salvific knowledge of God, but was completely darkened.

50. The will was subjected to the tyranny of sin and became its agent.

51. In this respect, men are said to be dead in sins (Col. 2:13).

52. By nature, they cannot do anything other than stink in sins and rot in the grave of sins.

53. Consequently, conversion is the work of God alone; man is purely passive in it.

54. It is God who opens the heart of man in conversion, softens it, circumcises it, and renews it.

55. It is God who not only perfects the work, but also works in man to will what is good (Phi. 2:13).

56. To be sure, man freely rules over his external motions, and therefore is able to provide a certain civil righteousness.

57. This in itself, from the classification of the act, is not sin; but since the person is not yet reconciled to God, nonetheless, sin is committed.[27]

58. So that the apostolic declaration remains ever firm: whatever is not from faith is sin (Rom. 14:23).

59. Accordingly, in order for works to be truly good before God, they must be done in a good manner, by good people, and for a good purpose.

---

27   κατ' ἄλλο *fit peccatum*.

60. For however much a certain freedom remains to the human will in external actions that relate to human life or even to the external exercise of religion—

61. Indeed, the apostle declares that the Gentiles do by nature the things that are of the Law (Rom. 2:14)—

62. Nevertheless, there do not remain in man the slightest powers for initiating spiritual motions and for providing worship that is pleasing to God.

63. For we are not fit to think anything good from ourselves, as being from ourselves, but our sufficiency is from God (2 Cor. 3:5).

64. Therefore, holy thoughts, good purposes, pious counsels, and all motives of a good will are from God. Through Him we are able to do something good. Without Him we can do nothing (Augustine, *de dogm. Eccles. cap. 17.*).

65. Nevertheless, that very freedom in external actions and in the works of the present life is not without its own hindrances and impediments.

66. Men often make plans. But God, who governs all things, often scatters their plans (Isaiah 8:10).

67. God disposes. It is only ours to propose. And what we wish for is often something other than a pious outcome.

68. In addition, great is the tyranny of Satan who, with God's permission, drags the will of the reprobate wherever he pleases, since their will has been entangled in the cords of sins.

69. The very multitude of responsibilities often disturbs the judgment of the mind and the decision of the will.

70. To these external impediments is added the inner feebleness of human powers, even in external matters, which has arisen from sin.

71. To this is joined the disorderliness of emotions, which is like a torrent, carrying the will away here and there and overturning the judgment of the mind.

72. This consideration of the powers that have been utterly lost in spiritual matters and weakened in external matters forces us to acknowledge the magnitude of the divine grace that converts and saves us. It casts all security from our hearts; it crushes the plumes of pride; it makes us more diligent in prayer and in safeguarding the gifts of the Spirit.

73. After conversion, the freed will of man is not idle, but is God's coworker, effectively using those new powers given from above.

74. That we may want that which is good, the Holy Spirit works in us, apart from us. And when we want it and want it in such a way that we do it, He cooperates with us.

75. For the sons of God are acted upon in such a way that they themselves also act (Augustine, *de corr. et grat. cap. 2.*).

76. This may be called a freedom from the slavery of sin, for where the Spirit of the Lord regenerates and illuminates a man, there is freedom (2 Cor. 3:17).

77. But that very freedom of the freed will perpetually requires the help and direction of the Holy Spirit.

78. Indeed, since in the reborn the flesh still struggles against the Spirit (Gal. 5:17), they are not yet free from all sin.

79. There is a free slavery in the spirit of the reborn, a servile freedom in the flesh of the reborn.

80. In the next life, they will finally obtain the full freedom of the will, when they will be free, not only from the slavery of sinning, but also from all sin altogether, from all misery, and from the danger of falling away.

81. This freedom may be called a freedom from sin and mutability.

82. In this freedom, they will not only not sin; they will not only be able not to sin; but they will also not be able to sin. May Christ, the Defender of our freedom, carry us on to that freedom.

Chapter 11: The Law

1. Word and Sacraments serve the restoration of man as the salutary antidotes to our spiritual disease.

2. There are two principal divisions of the Word: Law and Gospel.

3. The Law manifests the disease; but the Gospel shows the Physician.

4. The Law was given through Moses; but grace and truth come to us through Jesus Christ (John 1:17).

5. There are three kinds of Law given through Moses: moral, judicial, and ceremonial.

6. The moral law was merely repeated by Moses in solemn proclamation, for it was first engraved in the hearts of men.

7. Indeed, it is the mirror of God's eternal righteousness, the mirror of the pristine perfection of nature before the fall, the mirror of sin and of the inmost corruption of nature after the fall, the mirror of the obedience that is to be supplied by the reborn, the mirror of the perfection that will follow in the coming life.

8. Those who wish to eliminate this Law from the Church should themselves be eliminated.

9. For they speak against Christ, who made the explanation of the Law the preface to His preaching (Matthew 5–7).

10. They speak against the apostles, who preached repentance and the remission of sins in the name of Christ (Luke 24:47).

11. Indeed, the Law is the mirror of sin, not its remedy.

12. As long as the disease is not yet recognized, there is no desire for a remedy.

13. For the healthy have no need of a physician (Matthew 9:12), that is, those who think they are healthy, for in reality, all people are not only sick, but also dead in sins.

14. The Law is given that grace may be sought (Augustine, *de Spir. et lit. c. 19.*).

15. That which the Law demands, faith obtains (Augustine, *homil. 29. in Joh.*).

16. Through the Law is the knowledge of sin; the abolition of it is through faith (Ambrose, *in 3. cap. Rom.*).

17. Therefore, the ministry of death is necessary in order that life in Christ may be desired.

18. God does not pour out the oil of mercy except into a vessel that is broken and contrite.

19. He does not pardon sins, unless you acknowledge them; He does not cover them, unless you uncover them; He does not console, unless you are grieved.

20. The Law is the perfect way to eternal life, but it is weakened by the flesh (Rom. 8:3). For this reason, it is rendered to us ineffectual for life.

21. The Law is spiritual. It commands complete obedience, inwardly and outwardly, of body, soul, and spirit, throughout all parts of life. It demands spiritual actions, words, and thoughts. It requires a sound nature in every way.

22. But we are carnal (Rom. 7:14). We are flesh born of flesh (John 3:6). And we are not entirely freed in this life from the old flesh.

23. Consequently, we are not able to fulfill the Law in this life.

24. There is no man who does not sin (1 Kings 8:46). But sinning and fulfilling the Law are opposite things. Therefore, there is no man who fulfills the Law.

25. Therefore, every mouth is shut, and the whole world is made accountable to God (Rom. 3:19).

26. With the voice of the Law, God concludes all things under sin (Rom. 11:32; Gal. 3:22).

27. The standard of affirmative commandments is the First Commandment about fearing and loving God above all things.

28. The standard of negative commandments is the Last Commandment about not coveting (Augustine, *de perfect. justit.*).

29. Consequently, one does not satisfy the affirmative commandments with the mere beginning of the fear and love of God.

30. Nor does one satisfy the negative precepts by merely restraining oneself from external misdeeds.

31. Even if we make the most excellent beginning at external obedience and beware of external misdeeds, nevertheless, we always fall short in the First and Last Commandments.

32. But the express knowledge of the external and cruder crimes is made in the Decalogue in order that the human mind may understand from God's judgment how to judge the severity of the inner crimes.

33. Before God, an adulterer is not only the person who has relations with another's spouse, but also the person who covets the wife of another (Mat. 5:28).

34. Before God, a thief is not only the person who takes things from another against the other's will, but also the person who takes them by means of forbidden coveting.

35. Nor does God command only the hand and external members, but the whole man.

36. But who can say that his heart is clean of covetous desires? (Pro. 20:9.) Who, then, can boast that he is not a transgressor of the Law?

37. Therefore, the promises of the Law are useless to us.

38. But in Christ, they are yes and Amen (2 Cor. 1:20).

39. That which was impossible for the Law, God provided to us by sending His Son (Rom. 8:3).

40. But if righteousness comes through the Law, Christ died in vain (Gal. 2:21).

41. And if the reborn perfectly fulfill the Law, why do they daily pray for the forgiveness of debts, as Christ teaches and guides them? (Mat. 6:11.)

42. If no debt is contracted, why does he seek its remission?

43. The hands of Moses are heavy, and the yoke of the Law is unbearable (Exo. 17:12; Bernard, *serm. 3. in Cantic.*).

44. The face of Moses is radiant; we cannot gaze upon it (Exo. 34:29; 2 Cor. 3:13).

45. The tongue of Moses is heavy and inflexible; we cannot heed and obey his words (Exo. 4:10).

46. The tablets of the Decalogue are made of stone. They do not heal our heart; they crush it (Exo. 24:12).

47. It was Joshua, not Moses, who led the Israelites into the promised land. It is Christ, the heavenly Joshua, not Moses, who leads us to eternal life.

48. The Law is the hammer of death, the thunder of hell, the lightning of divine wrath.

49. The usefulness of the Law is that it convinces man of his infirmity and compels him to seek the medicine of grace, which is in Christ (Augustine, *Epist. 200. ad Asell.*).

50. Therefore, let us learn to recognize the voice of the Law, that we may recognize the characteristic voice of Christ our Shepherd.

51. Whatever shows sin, wrath, and death, exercises the office of the Law, whether it is done in the Old or the New Testament.

52. Let us not, then, assign the Law to the Old Testament and the Gospel to the New.

53. It is true that the solemn proclamation of the Law was made under the Old Testament, the Gospel in the New.

54. But the doctrine of both Law and Gospel sounded forth in both Testaments.

55. Nor did the knowledge of sin through the Law and the abolition of sin through faith in Christ appear only in the New Testament, but also in the Old.

56. But the ceremonial and forensic laws were abrogated in the New Testament.

57. For the former were a shadow and type of Christ. They expired when the body appeared.

58. The latter applied to the Jewish state, which God wanted to be enclosed in these boundaries until the coming of Christ.

59. But the abrogation of both the ceremonial and the forensic laws is such that what is of moral quality in them remains.

60. Indeed, the Mosaic ceremonies can be applied for our edification through allegorical exposition.

61. These things are said about the Law in general. There is a specific question concerning the numbering of the Decalogue and about images.

62. The cardinal numbering of the commandments of the Decalogue is certain, but not the ordinal numbering.

63. Therefore, it is a question, not of faith, but of the order of the commandments of the Decalogue.

64. For this reason, unnecessary controversies should not be started over this matter, so that well-established churches should be disturbed by them. Nor should it be permitted that Christian liberty be taken captive in these matters by the adversaries.

65. For the sake of the numbering used in our churches, we conclude thus: Whatever is a foreign god is prohibited by the First Commandment. The images to which divine worship is attributed are foreign gods. Therefore, they are prohibited by the First Commandment.

66. Nor is it absurd to say that there are two commandments about not coveting, for two kinds of coveting are condemned: actual and original.

67. For the foundations of this distinction can be proffered from Hebrew literature and from the apostolic writings.

68. Nor can it be said that the commandment about images is a special commandment established so that the use of them was simply prohibited.

69. For when the truth has been summoned, it can be proven with various documents that the use of images is affirmed.

70. Christian freedom permits historical images. The Law of God forbids images that are idolatrous, superstitious, and contaminated with marks of wantonness. Charity removes those that truly provide cause of offense.

71. As often as a notion of worship enters in, so that divine honor is conferred on images, whether it is thought that images have some peculiar holiness, or it is imagined that God is so bound to some image that there He is more attentive and effective than elsewhere, then the use of them is no longer an adiaphoron.

72. But we also have no praise for the conclusion of the Greek Pelusiota in Synod VII[28]: "There is no word of the temple that is not crowned with an image."

73. Nor do we approve of the abundance of costly images, lest that which Bernard bewails in *col. 1134* should happen, that the Church shines splendidly within her walls but is a beggar among the poor, that she covers her stones with gold but leaves her children naked, lest she serve the eyes of the rich at the expense of the needy.

74. Therefore, as with other adiaphora, so also in this area Christian prudence is required, lest we provide offense to the weak with the inopportune use of images, or, on the other hand, lest we yield to those who come in to attack the freedom which we have in Christ in order to return us to slavery (Gal. 2:4).

75. May He who once inscribed His Law on stone tablets with His finger inscribe it now on our hearts by His Spirit.

---

28 ναοῦ λόγος οὐδεὶς, ὃν οὐ στέφει ἄγαλμα.

Chapter 12: The Gospel

1. The Gospel is parallel to the Law.
2. The origin of both doctrines is heavenly.
3. Both promise eternal life, but in different ways.
4. The Law promises eternal life to those who are perfectly obedient; the Gospel, to those who believe in Christ.
5. Both doctrines are to be set forth in the Church.
6. For both have a necessary purpose in the conversion of a man.
7. Both are inseparably bound together in the heart and in the practice of the Christian man.
8. Nevertheless, these doctrines that are bound together must be carefully distinguished from one another.
9. For if their distinction is removed or even slightly shaken, the very stronghold of Christianity is demolished.
10. However, one must not introduce such a hostility between them that they mutually destroy one another.
11. For the Law is not opposed to the promises of God (Gal. 3:21).
12. But the Law is established through faith (Rom. 3:31).
13. The Gospel announces that what the Law requires of us has been provided by Christ in our place.
14. Christ, then, is the end and fulfillment of the Law for righteousness to everyone who believes (Rom. 10:4).
15. Through Christ the righteousness of the Law is fulfilled in us (Rom. 8:4).
16. Moreover, the faith that is kindled by the Holy Spirit through the word of the Gospel is effective through love (Gal. 5:6).

17. The summary of the Law is love (Rom. 13:10).

18. Indeed, in this way the Law is inscribed on hearts (Jer. 31:33).

19. But love is imperfect in this life.

20. Consequently, the obedience of the Law is also imperfect in this life.

21. Only the beginning is here. The fulfillment will follow in the life to come.

22. The Gospel, according to its name, is a good message.

23. For, in the counsel of the Most Holy Trinity, it announces that Christ, who is God and Man, has been made our Mediator and Redeemer.

24. It announces that Christ, by His most holy obedience, has perfectly satisfied the Law, and that He has merited for the whole world the grace of God, the remission of sins, the gift of the Holy Spirit, righteousness, and eternal life.

25. It announces that these benefits obtained by Christ are applied to believers and given by grace.

26. Therefore, because the preaching of this doctrine conveys the most bountiful material of joy, the prophets and apostles most worthily chose to use the words *Bisser* and εὐαγγελίζεσθαι in referring to it.

27. Some derive *Bisser* from *Basar*, flesh, which means to announce fleshy and tender things.

28. Others suggest, as the reason behind this name, that *Bisser* means to announce happy things to all flesh...

29. So that in this way the terms of this doctrine are indicated, that it offers its good things broadly to all people...

30. And so that the fate of its hearers may be expressed at the same time, that they are flesh and subject to many infirmities, and for this reason, they should by no means disregard this divinely offered salvation.

31. *Bisser* and εὐαγγελίζεσθαι are used when it is announced that enemies who were threatening great and imminent danger have been put to flight and that peace has been restored (1 Sam. 4:17; 1 Sam. 31:9; 2 Sam. 1:20; 2 Sam. 4:10; 2 Sam. 18:19).

32. Thus the Gospel announces that God has freed us from the hand of our enemies (Luke 2:74), rescued us from the power of darkness (Col. 1:13), plundered the principalities and powers, and triumphed over them (Col. 2:15).

33. *Bisser* and εὐαγγελίζεσθαι are also used when the birth of a son is announced to someone (Jer. 20:15).

34. Thus it is announced in the Gospel that to us a Child is born, to us a Son is given (Isa. 9:6), who has given to all who receive Him by faith the power to become sons of God (John 1:12), so that in this way the sonship may again come upon us through Him (Gal. 3:5).

35. Finally, these words are used when liberation is announced to the captives, consolation to those who grieve (Isa. 61:1–2).

36. Thus in the Gospel it is announced that Christ has led us, who were conquered, out of the lake in which there was no water (Zec. 9:11).

37. From here comes that most joyful acclamation in Isa. 40:1: Comfort, comfort My people, says your God, and speak to the heart of Jerusalem, and preach to her that her warfare is completed.

38. From this also flow those sweet names and phrases of this doctrine, that it is the Gospel of God's grace (Acts 20:24); the knowledge of salvation (Luke 1:77); the word of the kingdom (Mat. 13:19); the power of God for salvation to everyone who believes (Rom. 1:16); the word of life (Acts 5:20, Phi. 2:16); the word of eternal life (John 6:68); the word of salvation (Acts 13:26); the word of reconciliation (2 Cor. 5:19); the Law of the Spirit of life (Rom. 8:2); the Gospel of our salvation (Eph. 1:13); the promise of the inheritance (Rom. 4:13); a fountain of water welling up to eternal life (John 4:14); a pasture, a water of repose, a table, an over-

flowing cup, a rod, a staff (Psa. 23:2, 4, 5); an aroma of life (2 Cor. 2:15, etc.).

39. Consequently, that happy word 'Gospel' must not be transformed into the Law that accuses and terrifies.

40. They do this who argue that the Law teaches imperfect commandments about merely external works done out of fear, while the Gospel sets forth the more perfect, more excellent, and more weighty commandments.

41. As if the Law had not already previously been a yoke which our fathers were unable to bear (Acts 15:10); a yoke of burden, a staff of the shoulder and a rod of the oppressor (Isa. 9:6), so that we need a new law-giver?

42. Therefore, other differences must be sought between the Law and the Gospel, which the Scripture expresses in this way.

43. The Law is known, to a certain extent, by nature (Rom. 2:14–15). But the Gospel is a mystery entirely hidden from reason (Mat. 16:16, Rom. 16:25, 1 Cor. 2:7, Eph. 1:9).

44. The Law is a doctrine of works and a preacher of doing. The Gospel is a doctrine of faith and a preacher of that which has been done; that is, it announces that the things which the Law requires have been provided through Christ (Rom. 3:21, 4:5, 10:5).

45. The Law demands from everyone perfect obedience toward all God's commandments. But the Gospel teaches faith in Christ the Mediator.

46. The Law concludes under sin (Gal. 3:22). It makes the whole world guilty before God (Rom. 3:19). It works wrath (Rom. 4:15). It places under a curse (Gal. 3:10). Consequently, it is a ministry of death and condemnation. The Gospel is a word of salvation, peace, and reconciliation.

47. Therefore, both doctrines revolve around sin, but in different ways.

48. The Law shows, accuses, and condemns sin. However,

the Gospel shows Him who made satisfaction for sin, and thus it covers, removes, and remits sin.

49. The promises of the Law require perfect obedience of works. But the promises of the Gospel are free.

50. Therefore, the promises of the Law are useless to us (Heb. 7:18), that is, because of the defect of our flesh (Rom. 8:3). But in Christ, the promises of God are made and fulfilled (2 Cor. 1:20).

51. The Law shows which works are good, but it does not confer the powers to do them. The Gospel contains the promise of the renewal of the Spirit, who writes the Law into our hearts (Jer. 31:33).

52. Therefore, these are all benefits of the Gospel: justification and renewal, grace and the gift by grace, the imputation of the righteousness of Christ, and the giving of the Holy Spirit.

53. And yet they must not be confused. Justification must not be located in renewal, which is the consequence of justification, not the cause.

54. For God does not receive us into grace and justify us on account of the renewal and the beginning of obedience. Instead, He renews by the Holy Spirit those who have been justified and received into grace, so that they are able to begin obeying the Law.

55. The Gospel shows that this beginning of obedience in those who are righteous by faith in Christ is pleasing to God, even though it is imperfect and tainted in many ways.

56. The Law should be set before the hypocrites and the secure. The Gospel should be set before the broken and contrite.

57. The Law coerces the Old Man. The Gospel retains the New Man under grace.

58. And since the reborn are not entirely freed from the old flesh in this life, but the struggle between flesh and Spirit remains in them (Gal. 5:17), they are also in need of the ministry of the Law.

59. And for this reason, the Law exercises itself in these works with a twofold goal, both that the flesh, that is, the Old Man, may be coerced in them, and that the New Man may learn.

60. Besides this, it must by all means be noted that these promises of the Gospel are universal in a twofold manner, both because of time and also because of the object.

61. By universality of time, we understand that it is one and the same Gospel by which all the saints of all times have been saved since the beginning of the world.

62. Jesus Christ is the same yesterday and today, even forever (Heb. 13:8). Therefore, the suffering of Christ was beneficial before it happened.

63. For the Lamb was slain from the beginning of the world (Rev. 13:8); that is, with regard to the eternal decree, with regard to the promises, with regard to the types, and with regard to the efficacy.

64. Therefore, we believe with the apostles that we are saved by the grace of God, just as our fathers were (Acts 15:8).

65. Nor is it only in the New Testament, but also in the Old, that those who seek righteousness and salvation in the works of the Law are under a curse (Gal. 3:10).

66. Immediately after the fall, the promise was added about the Seed of the woman who would crush the head of the serpent (Gen. 3:15), which was the protevangel by which our first parents were sustained.

67. The great Martin Chemnitz (in *part 2. locor. p. 579. et. seq.*) very beautifully expounds how this promise was explained more clearly in later times and repeated through the divine revelation that was given to the patriarchs and prophets.

68. And just as there is one Gospel, so there is one faith, one manner of obtaining righteousness and salvation.

69. Therefore, it is a false notion that, before the time of Moses, men were saved by the Law of nature; after the age of Moses, by the

Levitical Law; and in the New Testament, by the Evangelical Law.

70. Also false is the idea that there is an equal distribution of Law in the Old Testament and of the Gospel in the New, in this sense, that whatever is set forth in the Old Testament pertains to the Law, and whatever is set forth in the New Testament pertains to the Gospel.

71. For the Gospel was promised beforehand through the prophets in the Holy Scriptures (Rom. 1:2) and all the prophets give witness to Christ, that those who believe in His name receive the remission of sins (Acts 10:43).

72. Briefly, what the prophets predicted as a future event, the apostles announced as something completed.

73. With the universality of the object we understand that the promises of the Gospel pertain to all men.

74. But here we distinguish between the promise and the application of the promise. The promise has absolutely all men in view, but the application of the promise is for believers only.

75. For here the question is not whether all people are actually made partakers of the benefits which are offered through the word of the Gospel. For, sadly, the matter itself bears witness that such is not the case.

76. But the question is whether the promises of the Gospel are universal in and of themselves, or whether they are restricted in such a way that, by the counsel and decree of God, they only pertain to certain men who were absolutely elected before others by His good pleasure.

77. Here we say that God seriously desires the salvation of all men, that Christ made satisfaction for absolutely all men, and, therefore, that God seriously offers the benefits of Christ to all men through the Gospel.

78. Christ orders the Gospel to be preached to every creature (Mark 16:15). Therefore, He commands the apostles to preach

to everyone everywhere and to offer the Gospel; in the Gospel, the benefits of His suffering and death; in the benefits of His suffering and death, the remission of sins; in the remission of sins, the grace of God; in the grace of God, salvation and eternal life.

79. Therefore, whoever believes—that is, the one who, by the faith which the Holy Spirit wants to work by means of this very word of the Gospel in all who hear and do not stubbornly resist, receives the offered gifts—will be saved (Mark 16:16).

80. To all, therefore, God offers the Gospel to this end, that by hearing it, they may conceive faith, with contrition as the forerunner and good works following after, which are the fruit of the renewal and faith kindled by the Holy Spirit.

81. By means of His consequent and judicial will, the preaching of the Gospel becomes to some the aroma of death to death (2 Cor. 2:15).

82. Concerning this universality of object, it must be noted that it does not exclude, but rather includes faith.

83. For faith and the promise are correlative.

84. Therefore, the doctrine of the Gospel is called the word of faith (Rom. 10:8, 1 Tim. 4:6), the hearing and preaching of faith (Gal. 3:2).

85. This condition of faith is not etiological; the promises of the Law are conditional in this way. Rather, it is syllogistic, for the manner and instrument is being expressed by which we embrace the promised good things.

86. The word of the Law is that, if you obey perfectly, you will be saved. In this case, the condition is etiological, because perfect obedience is the cause on account of which[29] eternal life is given to those who keep the Law.

87. The word of the Gospel is that, if you believe, you will be saved. In this case, the condition is syllogistic, because the Gospel

---

29 *causa propter quam*

declares that we are justified before God and saved, not on account of faith, but through faith, which lays hold of Christ.

88. It can easily be understood from the definition of the Gospel whether the Gospel, properly speaking, is a preaching of repentance.

89. When the Gospel is understood generally as the whole doctrine which Christ and the apostles preached, it is certainly true that the Gospel is a preaching of repentance.

90. Besides, the Gospel announces the grace of God only to the penitent; that is, to those who have been humbled by the recognition of sins and by a sense of divine wrath.

91. Indeed, in declaring that salvation must be sought in Christ alone, it presupposes that all things outside of Christ have been concluded under sin.

92. Moreover, the Gospel demonstrates certain explanations of the Law, which a person could not easily and evidently gather from the Law alone.

93. In this sense, then, and in these respects, the Gospel can be called and can be rightly understood to be a preaching of repentance. At the same time, the proper doctrine of the Gospel continues to be the free remission of sins on account of Christ.

94. You say: Faith is from the Gospel; therefore, unbelief is also reproved by the Gospel, for the Law does not know Christ the Mediator.

95. We reply: The Law demands that every word of God be believed. The Gospel supposes this word of God, that Christ died on the cross for us, that Christ is our righteousness before God. Let the Law conclude: You should believe this word of God.

96. The Law reproves all sins, and thus also unbelief. The Gospel shows in its antithesis that this is sin, and indeed, the chief of all sins, not to believe in Christ the Mediator, as Chemnitz teaches (*p. 2. loc. pag. 570.*). The Law concludes: You should be reproved and condemned on account of that sin.

97. In this sense Dr. Luther said in *cap. 2. Gal.* that the Law and Gospel are, in practice, more closely bound together than any mathematical point.

98. And, nevertheless, the proper office of the Law is still to reprove sin, to work wrath, to condemn; while the proper office of the Gospel is to comfort, to raise up, to save.

99. When the Law sets forth its major premise, that whoever has stolen is under a curse, the conscience of the thief assumes, I have stolen. The Law concludes: You are under a curse.

100. There the entire accusing and condemning syllogism is attributed to the Law, even though the conscience of the thief adds the assumption.

101. So also the Law sets forth its major premise: Whoever is under sin is cursed. The Gospel sets forth the minor premise: Whoever does not believe in the Son is still under sin, and the wrath of God remains on him (John 3:36). The Law concludes: Therefore, he is cursed.

102. There likewise the entire accusing and condemning syllogism should be attributed to the Law, even though the doctrine of the Gospel adds the assumption.

103. The Law concludes all under sin (Gal. 3:22). Therefore, whoever does not believe the Gospel, which shows Christ, remains under the Law's curse, and against him the Law exercises its office of accusing and condemning, with all its vigor and rigor.

104. The accusation, then, of unbelief pertains to the Law as it has been illuminated by the light of the Gospel.

105. For this reason, Dr. Luther writes in *Genes. c. 22. f. 303.* that the work of faith in Christ and the opposite sin of unbelief both go back to the First Commandment.

106. May the Lord Jesus, by the word of the Gospel, effectively sustain and build up our hearts in the face of all temptations, especially in the hour of death.

Chapter 13: Repentance

1. The practice of Law and Gospel consists in repentance.

2. For it is not enough to know what the office of the Law or the Gospel is; it is necessary to practice each. Theology is practical doctrine.

3. Repentance is ascribed either to God or to men.

4. It is ascribed to God anthropopathically, not theopathically; actively, not passively.

5. For as the wrath of God is not the disturbance of His spirit, but the judgment by which the penalty for sin is imposed, so His repentance is the immutable disposition of things that must be changed (Augustine, *15. de Civitat. Dei cap. 25.*).

6. God does not think as men think, so that some new idea occurs to Him; nor does He become angry as if He were mutable. No, such things are read so that the severity of our sins may be expressed (Ambrose, *lib. de arca et Noah cap. 4.*).

7. Repentance is ascribed to men in a far different sense than it is to God. For God is not like man, that He should repent of anything (1 Sam. 15:29).

8. When repentance is ascribed to man, it is used in the Scriptures in two ways, either wholly or partially.

9. Wholly, for the entire act of conversion; partially, for contrition only.

10. The force of the word leans more toward the second meaning. For 'to repent' means for a person to be ashamed and upset over something he has done (Gell., *17. c. 1.*)

11. But the use of Scripture and of our churches leans more toward the first meaning.

12. For this reason, some of the fathers found the word *'resipiscentia'*—a change of mind—to be more accurate (Tertullian, *2. contra Marc. Lactant. 6. Inst. c. 24.*).

13. The Hebrews most accurately call it *Theschubah*, which the Greeks translate ἐπιστροφή, and which we call 'conversion.'

14. Phavorinus explains this beautifully. He says it means the turning away from misdeeds to the opposite good.

15. By that one should understand good itself, the highest good.

16. For this reason, Damascenus puts it very beautifully. He says it is a turning back from that which is contrary to nature to that which is according to nature, and from the devil to God (*2. de Orth. fide. 30.*).

17. What we call 'repentance,' the Greeks call μεταμέλεια καὶ μετάνοια.

18. In such a way, though, that μεταμέλεια corresponds to repentance understood as contrition alone, which is a sorrow of the spirit that is not combined with faith (Heb. 4:2). But μετάνοια corresponds to repentance as it is generally understood, which is a sorrow leading to salvation, not to be regretted (2 Cor. 7:10).

19. It is clear that this distinction is not always made. (Cf. Mat. 21:29 and Heb. 12:17.)

20. Generally, however, μετάνοια denotes true and salutary repentance, while μεταμέλεια denotes a false and destructive repentance.

21. There are two kinds of false repentance. One is hypocritical, consisting in only an external appearance and pretense. The prophet calls this 'theatrical,' which Christ meant to express when He said that some fast (and mourn) to make a public show, so that they are seen by men (Mat. 6:16).

22. The other kind is incomplete and mutilated, lamenting sin, but without grace and faith.

23. But true and salutary repentance consists in genuine contrition and faith.

24. Some call this repentance 'evangelical,' where the explanation is to be added that it is so named on account of the weightier part, namely, faith, which is of the Gospel.

25. This true repentance is a movement of the heart, kindled by the Holy Spirit, in which the man who has acknowledged his sins and God's wrath against them seriously grieves, and, by faith in Christ, who made satisfaction for sins, he builds himself up again, being firmly convinced that his sins are forgiven him for Christ's sake.

26. For repentance is conversion from darkness to light, from the power of Satan to God (Acts 26:18).

27. Therefore, the *terminus a quo* is sin; from a consideration of sin, contrition arises. The *terminus ad quem* is God, to whose mercy the way lies open through the merit of Christ.

28. As many kinds of heavenly doctrine as there are, by whose ministry God preaches to men repentance and the remission of sins and works these things in men, so many are its essential parts. But there are two kinds of heavenly doctrine; namely, Law and Gospel. Therefore, there are two parts of repentance.

29. Each of these doctrines has its peculiar and proper effect in converting a man. The Law instills sorrow, as it manifests sins and God's wrath against them. The Gospel comforts, as it sets forth to the contrite man Christ the Mediator, the Lamb of God who takes away the sins of the world.

30. These effects of Law and Gospel may be distinct, but they work together to carry out the single purpose of repentance.

31. With the Scriptures as our guide, we call good works, that is, new obedience, not a part of repentance, but fruits worthy of repentance (Luke 3:8; Acts 26:20).

32. Some argue that the mortification of the flesh and the vivification of the spirit are parts of repentance.

33. We do not object to this, if by 'mortification' they mean contrition, that is, the sorrow conceived from the recognition of sins and from a sense of divine wrath; and if by 'vivification' they mean the comfort which comes from faith.

34. But if they mean that perpetual zeal on the part of the converted and reborn in mortifying the Old Man and in pursuing the fruits of the Spirit, then we say that this all pertains to new obedience.

35. Since new obedience is not perfect in this life, the whole life of a Christian man is perpetual repentance (Dr. Luther in his first propositions concerning indulgences, thesis 1.)

36. The three parts of repentance, as it is sometimes divided—the contrition of the heart, the confession of the mouth, and the satisfaction of the work—have their place, not in that salutary and internal conversion toward God wherein we deal with God, but in that public ecclesiastical repentance employed among the fathers.

37. For long ago, if someone caused a scandal for the other Christians with his public crimes, and therefore was excluded from the ecclesiastical assembly, there were required of him public proofs of repentance, besides the internal contrition of the heart, namely, grieving, confession, supplication, etc., by which he was to make satisfaction to the Church. (Blessed Rhenanus in *scholiis ad Tertull. de poenit.*).

38. Therefore, those who want these parts to belong to that salutary repentance by which we deal with God abuse this division.

39. For faith can by no means be excluded from it. Indeed, without faith, repentance cannot be repentance to life (Acts 11:18).

40. Tears are good, as long as you acknowledge Christ (Ambrose, in *cap. 24. Luc. 17.*).

41. But a far worse patch is added, if those actions of the penitent person are thought to obtain the reason of origin or material, not only signifying but also causing and effecting the remission

of sins in the sacrament of penance, with which the voice of the absolving confessor agrees as a formality, of which very thing there is a remarkable discrepancy among writers. (See the comments on 4. sent. dist. 14.)

42. Even though Scripture ascribes the remission of sins to Christ and His merit, apprehended by faith, it is really ascribed, according to this false understanding, to our zeal and merit.

43. Contrition is required in conversion, not as a cause and merit of reconciliation with God, but by way of sequence.

44. Indeed, Christ preaches the Gospel, but He preaches it to the poor; He heals, but He heals the contrite in heart; He preaches remission of sins, but He preaches it to the captives; He preaches sight, but He preaches it to the blind; He preaches forgiveness, but He preaches it to the broken, that is, to those who acknowledge their spiritual poverty, captivity, and blindness and who, because of it, are of a broken and contrite heart (Isa. 61:1; Luke 4:18).

45. All these things pertain to such contrition: a recognition of sin, a sense of divine wrath, the grief and anguish of a fearful conscience, the hatred of and the fleeing from sin; and also external signs of contrition: tears, fasting, beating of the breast, sackcloth, etc.

46. Furthermore, there is a difference between the contrition of the godly and that of the ungodly and the hypocrites.

47. The contrition of the godly arises from the special operation of the Holy Spirit. But the contrition of the ungodly and hypocrites has its origin, for the most part, in the Old Man and the natural powers of free will.

48. The godly, in pangs of conscience, have God Himself in view as the principal object of their sin, and they grieve especially for their offense against Him. The hypocrites esteem rather the judgments of their own mind or of others, and they are troubled more by a consideration of the penalty than of the guilt.

49. The godly have in view not only actual sins, but also the fount of all actual sins, namely, the original stain; not only outward sins, but also the inner corruption; not only the penalties of the present life, but also of the life to come. But the hypocrites only acknowledge outward sins to some degree. And as they are greatly alarmed even by the penalties of this life, if they do rise up to a consideration of eternal penalties, they are carried off to the abyss of despair.

50. The godly acknowledge and confess that God and His judgments are just. It is common for the hypocrites to minimize their crimes and to criticize the justice of God.

51. At the same time, it is wrong for us to think of one kind of contrition that is from the Law, and another kind that is from the Gospel.

52. For that very contrition of the godly (which they call 'evangelical') is from the Law, not from the Gospel.

53. God often adds to the sermon of the Law real and visible sermons about sins and the greatness of His wrath, namely, public and private calamities, both among us and among others.

54. For to this end God sends the punishments of this life, that He may lead us to a recognition and hatred of sin (1 Cor. 10:22).

55. The doctrine of contrition is twisted, if it is denied that it is a part of repentance and a terror conceived from the threats of the Law, while it is asserted, on the other hand, that sorrow over sins is taken up voluntarily.

56. Likewise if it is taught that man (still existing in his old state) truly cooperates in conversion; that contrition pertains mainly to the Gospel; that it is a cause of the remission of sins; that the purpose of living well is also included in it, etc.

57. All these things are asserted and defended contrary to the Scripture and truth.

58. As for the things that are disputed among the scholastics concerning the appreciatively and intensively greatest sorrow, and likewise, that the sorrow over sin should exceed or equal the pleasure conceived over sin, etc., we say that such things have become the torturers of souls.

59. Contrition is certainly required; not a hypocritical or superficial contrition, but one that is genuine and from the whole heart.

60. But God forbid we should say that it can be equal to the magnitude, either of sin, or of the wrath of God, or of the penalties.

61. God is the infinite Good who has been offended. Sin is the infinite evil which has been committed. Penalty is the infinite misfortune that has been obtained.

62. How, then, could the infinite God, His infinite justice, His infinite wrath toward sins, be expiated with a finite contrition?

63. The doctrine of faith is no less twisted when it is denied that it is a part of repentance; when it is denied that faith is confidence; when it is denied that faith is certainty of the remission of sins; when it is denied that the principal object of faith is the Gospel promises about Christ the Mediator; when it is denied that faith alone justifies; when it is denied that faith is inseparable from love, etc.

64. These things are erroneous concerning confession: that it is required by divine Law that a declaration of all the sins which a person remembers, after diligent meditation and strict examination, must be made to the ears of a priest; that by such confession sin is wiped out; and that by the minor shame which those making confessing suffer before the priest, the immense shame is atoned for, which they would otherwise suffer on the Day of Judgment, etc.

65. But they oppose one another here with various arguments. Some extend this command to venial sins, others to mortal sins alone. Some seek its origin in divine Law, others in the constitution of the Church. Some extend the power of contrition to

the remission of guilt, others to the remission of penalty, either in whole or in part. (On this whole matter, see Biel. 4. sent. dist. 17. q. 1.)

66. We say that private confession is extremely useful, both on account of the ministry of the Church and also on account of those making confession.

67. For in this way, one can guard against admitting the unworthy to the use of the Holy Supper; delinquents can be corrected; the lethargic can be spurred on; the forgiveness of sins can be announced to the terrified; counsel can be given to those in doubt; and the more uneducated can be taught.

68. Therefore, Master Philip spoke rightly in his explanation of the Gospel for *Misericordias Domini*, the second[30] Sunday after Easter, which he spoke to his hearers in the last year of his life: Cherish that custom of private absolution! For if that custom were abolished, what would the Church be like? That custom stands as a witness that there is forgiveness of sins in the Church.

69. Nor do we disapprove of an enumeration of the sins with which the conscience is greatly troubled.

70. And yet we strenuously deny that an enumeration of all sins is necessary by divine Law.

71. Nor do we acknowledge any merit in confession, in obtaining the forgiveness of sins.

72. They teach a certain kind of satisfaction by which one may make satisfaction, either for guilt or at least for the temporal penalty of sins, but that such penalties can be relaxed or removed by indulgences, and that if one does not make full satisfaction, he must sweat in purgatory.

73. We acknowledge no other satisfaction but the satisfaction of Christ, and we affirm that sins are freely remitted to those who are truly penitent, on account of that satisfaction of Christ.

---

30   in explic. Evang. mis. Dom. I. post Pascha

74. The troubles imposed on the godly after their reconciliation with God are not properly penalties of an angry God as if He were a severe Judge. Rather, they are fatherly reproofs.

75. These are not imposed to that end, as if through them repayment or satisfaction could be made for sins, but that the godly may hate sin all the more; that the fear of God may increase in them; that security may be cast out, lest they offend God with new sins; that they may mortify the flesh with its covetous desires; that they may be a witness to the fact that they would perish eternally if they weren't received into grace by the Son, the Mediator; that they may be humbled under the mighty hand of God; that the others may be admonished about God's judgment against sins.

76. Briefly, in order that they may grow in patience, hope, desire for eternal life, prayer, the mortification of the Old Adam, etc.

77. Nazianzus puts it beautifully concerning these troubles of the godly when he says that they are bitter arrows from the sweet hand of God.

78. These things are said concerning the repentance which, with Lactantius, we rightly call a 'haven of salvation' (6. *div. Instit. c.* 24.). Knowing our weakness, God has, in His faithfulness, opened to man a haven of salvation, in order that the medicine of repentance may come to the aid of this need to which our fragility has been subjected.

79. Lest we put off repenting, a good many things should invite us: Access to the grace of God lies open to us only through repentance.

80. The impenitent heart treasures up for itself divine wrath, and the impenitent life is a devilish slavery.

81. We are not certain of even one more day of life. Why, then, should repentance be put off till tomorrow?

82. The angels rejoice over those who repent. They must, then, undoubtedly mourn over those who put off repenting until tomorrow.

83. Late-in-the-day repentance is seldom genuine, and when people persevere till the end of their life in sins, it is not they who leave the sins, but the sins which leave them behind.

84. May the Lord convert us, that we may be converted, and may He Himself work in us by His Spirit what we cannot do of ourselves.

Chapter 14: The Faith by Which We Are Justified before God

1. Faith is the second part of repentance. It is not only knowledge and assent, but also trust.

2. The terms used by Scripture to refer to faith, such as knowing, wisdom, understanding, light, recognition, etc., show that faith is knowledge.

3. Nor can the trust of the heart be placed in an object that is unknown to the mind.

4. Farewell, then, to that implicit faith by which Christians are assisted in that labor of testing the spirits (1 John 4:1), and watching out for false prophets (Mat. 7:15).

5. Farewell to the fictional notion that faith is more rightly defined as ignorance than as knowledge.

6. For even if faith is not knowledge deduced from and built upon the principles of reason, nevertheless, it is the light of knowledge that has arisen from the revelation of God through the Gospel. In this light we see light (Psa. 36:11).

7. It is evident that faith is assent and agreement. For it is not enough to know what God has revealed; one must also give assent to those things as being divinely revealed.

8. The terms used by Scripture to refer to faith—such as substance, full assurance, confidence, and boldness—show that faith is trust.

9. The descriptions of faith in practice show the same thing. The faith of Abraham is described in this way: that he believed in hope against hope (Rom. 4:18); that he was not weakened in faith (v. 19); that he did not hesitate with distrust toward the promise of

God, but, being made firm in faith, gave glory to God (v. 20); that he was firmly convinced that God was able to do whatever things He promised (v. 21).

10. The faith of the woman with a bleeding disorder, which Christ praises, is described in this way: that she said in her heart, If I touch His cloak, I will be healed (Mat. 9:22).

11. The faith of the Canaanite woman, the greatness of which Christ proclaims, is described in this way: that she struggled, as in a wrestling match, with the temptation concerning the delay of help, concerning the specificity of the promises, and concerning her own unworthiness (Mat. 15:28).

12. Thus faith receives Christ (John 1:12). It is the spiritual pasture of the soul (John 4:14; John 6:35; Rev. 21:6). It is the seal of the divine promises (John 3:33). It is the view of Christ hanging on the cross (John 3:15). These things certainly cannot be attributed to a bare knowledge.

13. In addition, consider the things that are contrasted with it in the same context. Not only is ignorance contrasted with faith, together with a darkened understanding, but also little faith and cowardice (Mat. 8:26); doubt (Mat. 14:31); fear (Luke 8:25); the wavering of unbelief (Rom. 4:20).

14. With regard to the knowledge and assent of faith, the adequate object is the Word of God contained in the prophetic and apostolic writings.

15. Beyond the sphere of this object, no matter what it is, it cannot be the foundation of faith.

16. Consequently, far be it from us to allow ourselves to be persuaded to receive traditions with the same sense of godliness as we do the written Word of God.

17. Nor will human reason be the measure of faith, but it must rather be conformed to the rule of the Word. For every thought must be taken captive to the obedience of Christ (2 Cor. 10:5).

18. With regard to trust, the adequate object of faith is Christ the Mediator and Redeemer, or (which is the same thing) the promise of the Gospel concerning the satisfaction and merit of Christ.

19. Meanwhile, we do not deny that faith also apprehends the promises about other blessings, both spiritual and physical. But faith in such things does not justify.

20. For it is first necessary for a person to rely on Christ, to seek reconciliation with God in Him and through Him, before he is able to apply other promises of God to himself.

21. For in Christ alone are all the promises of God 'yes' and 'Amen' (2 Cor. 1:20).

22. Moreover, faith justifies, insofar as it apprehends the merit of Christ offered to it in the word of the Gospel.

23. There are different kinds of things set forth before us in the Scripture to be believed. Meanwhile, Christ in His office of redemption is the goal of the whole Scripture, about whom it is written in the scroll of the book (Psa. 40:7).

24. So also faith assents to the whole Word of God in such a way that it considers especially the promise of grace set forth in the Gospel.

25. And if faith is trust that relies on the merit of Christ, it follows that the man who truly believes in Christ can and should know with certainty that his sins are also forgiven him for the sake of Christ, that he has a propitious God, and that he will inherit life.

26. All these things clearly argue in favor of this: the firmness of the divine promises, the dependability of the divine oath, the truth of the Holy Spirit as He witnesses and seals, the usefulness of the Sacraments, the infallibility of the promise to hear, and the character of true faith.

27. To this pertains that excellent passage of Bernard, *serm. 3. de fragm. sept. miser.* Three things I consider in which all my hope

consists: the love of adoption, the truthfulness of the promise, and the power of execution. Let my foolish thoughts murmur all they wish, saying, Who are you? And how great is that glory? And by what merits do you hope to obtain it? And I shall answer confidently: I know whom I have believed, and I am certain that He has adopted me in love that is too great, that He is truthful in what He promises, that He is powerful in carrying it out. This is the cord of three strands that is hard to break. It has been dropped down for us from our fatherland even into this prison. Therefore, I beg, let us firmly hold onto it, that it may come to our aid, that it may draw us upward to view the glory of the great God.

28. That true and saving faith is a free gift of God (Eph. 2:8, Phi. 1:29); the working of God (Col. 2:12); whose Author and Perfecter is Christ (Heb. 12:2).

29. Consequently, faith is not the merit of works that come first, but the foundation of the works that follow.

30. But God does not work faith in men's hearts immediately. Instead, the Holy Spirit, through the word of the Gospel, like a heavenly lamp, kindles the light of faith in our hearts, which are dark by nature. Rom. 10:17: Faith comes by hearing, and hearing by the Word of God.

31. To the Word are added the Sacraments also, which are likewise a means of begetting and nurturing faith.

32. Consequently, to wait for heavenly raptures, outside of and in addition to the Word, belongs to those who will not be content with the means instituted by God.

33. True faith—the faith that the Holy Spirit has worked in our hearts through the living Word of God (Heb. 4:12)—is not dead (James 2:17).

34. On the contrary, faith is active and effective (Gal. 5:6).

35. That activity of faith is twofold. In the first activity, it relies on Christ the Mediator, shown by the Word of the Gospel, and appre-

hends His benefits; in the second, it is effective through love.

36. When we say, then, that faith justifies—and indeed, faith alone—then both propositions must be explained.

37. Faith justifies, not because of its worthiness and excellence, nor because of the activity that follows, but because it apprehends Christ the Mediator.

38. Therefore, there is no real discrepancy between these things, if some say that faith justifies instrumentally, while others say that it justifies formally.

39. In the first manner, faith is understood as a gift of God, kindled in the heart by the Gospel, as a believing heart, and thus it is the instrument by which Christ is apprehended.

40. In the second manner, faith is understood as the very apprehension of Christ through faith, and thus it is the formal cause; that is, the reason and the manner of our justification.

41. But neither is there any real discrepancy, if some say that it is faith that justifies formally, while others say that it is Christ, and others, that it is the merit of Christ.

42. For in the same way, it is as if you said that the faith which apprehends Christ justifies, or that Christ is our righteousness before God which is apprehended by a true faith, or that the merit of Christ is imputed to us through faith for righteousness.

43. For the proper object of saving faith is Christ with His merit, and Christ, in turn, is of no benefit to us unless His righteousness is imputed to us through faith.

44. Properly speaking, then, the formal cause of our justification is the righteousness of Christ; that is, His active and passive obedience, apprehended by faith and divinely imputed to us. We must think about this matter in the following way.

45. God, in His judgment, demands an accounting of the gifts that were granted to us; that is, of His perfection and integrity with which He had created us in His own image.

46. But He does not find that concreated integrity, discernment, and righteousness in us. Instead, He finds sin and iniquity, because of which we are accused and condemned by the Law, which is the standard of righteousness.

47. Here, then, enters into the courtroom the gratuitous mercy of God, which offers us Christ the Mediator and Redeemer. He takes from us that which is ours, namely, sin and iniquity, and He gives us that which is His, namely, the obedience which He presented to the Law.

48. From this foundation, God, who is at once merciful and righteous, with great temperance, does not impute sin to us, but instead imputes to us the righteousness of Christ, namely, through the faith which relies and depends on Christ as the Mercy Seat.

49. This imputation of the righteousness of Christ through faith is as true and real as the fact that Christ truly took our iniquities upon Himself (Isa. 53:4).

50. The remission of sins is founded on the righteousness of Christ. For God does not remit sins by mistake, or by ignorance, or by fickleness, or by carelessness, but on account of Christ, whom faith apprehends.

51. And thus in justification the justice and the mercy of God are laid bare. His justice shines in the most perfect satisfaction made by Christ for our sins. His mercy is manifest in accepting Christ's satisfaction and applying it through faith.

52. In turn, the imputation of the righteousness of Christ results in sins that are remitted, because the guilt of the person cannot stand together with the imputation of the righteousness of Christ.

53. Consequently, as original sin is not only the lack of original righteousness, but also a depraved concupiscence, so also our justification before God consists in the remission of sins and the imputation of Christ's righteousness.

54. Renewal is closely joined to that remission of sins, imputation of the righteousness of Christ, regeneration, and adoption, for Christ does not only give us His righteousness, but also the Holy Spirit who renews our nature.

55. Nevertheless, our justification before God does not consist in both things at once.

56. But that renewal is the result of justification, and since it is never full and perfect in this weakness of nature, we cannot ascribe to it the glory of the righteousness that stands before God's judgment.

57. Indeed, this is exactly what we mean when we say that we are justified by faith 'alone.'

58. Where the particle 'alone' does not limit the subject, as if justifying faith were alone, separated from love and the other virtues.

59. Indeed, true faith is living, not dead. It is effective through love, not without works.

60. But that exclusive particle limits what is preached in this sense, that only the righteousness of Christ—of whom the power of apprehending belongs to faith alone, not to works—is imputed to us for righteousness.

61. Therefore, we do not deny that the Holy Spirit kindles new motives in the reborn or that the justified walk in good works.

62. In fact, we expressly declare that, where those new motives have not yet been stirred up by the Holy Spirit, there also true faith has not yet been kindled. We expressly declare that good works should follow in those who have been justified.

63. That said, we most surely deny, either that those new motives are a habitual righteousness that avails before God, or that those good works are the actual righteousness on which we can rely before the judgment seat of God.

64. Instead, the certainty of all our trust is in the precious blood of Christ (Augustine, in *Meditat.*).

65. For woe to the life of men, however laudable it may be, if he should plead his case apart from the mercy of God. (Augustine, in *Meditat. lib. 9. Confess. cap. 13.*).

66. Let us, then, urge the exclusive particles in the merit, in the application, and in the form of justification.

67. In other words, let us not think of works either as the merit, or as the means, or as the form of our justification before God.

68. But only the grace of God, for the sake of Christ alone, whom faith alone apprehends, justifies us.

69. The goal of that saving faith is the salvation of our souls and eternal life (1 Pet. 1:8).

70. For not only do we have access through faith to grace, but by faith we also stand in grace (Rom. 5:1) and by the power of God we are kept for salvation through faith (1 Pet. 1:5).

71. And yet, although faith can be separated from love as little as sunbeams from the sun or heat from fire, nevertheless, far be it from us to claim that faith is formed through love.

72. For faith is said to be dead apart from works, not as if works were its soul, but because that profession and boast of faith which does not have the testimony of good works is a likeness without any life, much like a cadaver.

73. Therefore, works are the witness of true faith, just as breathing testifies to a man's life. But they themselves are not the life of faith.

74. Just as good fruits testify to the goodness of a tree, but do not themselves make the tree good.

75. It rightly follows, then, that among the causes on account of which good works are to be done, faith is also numbered, lest faith and the Holy Spirit should be excluded.

76. For the Scripture testifies with sayings and examples that those who have truly been justified before God by faith in

Christ, if they afterward indulge in sins against their conscience, lose that faith and, as a result, also the grace of God, righteousness, the Holy Spirit, and eternal salvation. What is more, they fall into eternal condemnation, unless they are again converted to God by true repentance.

77. Therefore, let the apostolic warnings always sound in our ears and hearts: Work out your salvation with fear and trembling (Phi. 2:12). He who thinks he stands, let him see to it that he does not fall (1 Cor. 10:12). Be diligent to make your call and election sure (2 Pet. 1:10). Examine yourselves, whether you are in the faith. Test yourselves. Do you not know yourselves, that Christ Jesus is in you? Unless, perhaps, you are reprobates (2 Cor. 13:5).

78. May the Lord Jesus, the Author of our faith, be also its Perfecter (Heb. 12:2). To Him be the glory forever!

Chapter 15: Good Works

That is, the renewal of the man who has been born again through faith in Christ

1. Renewal is joined to regeneration and adoption through faith in Christ with a perpetual and indivisible bond.

2. For just as man, through carnal birth, is rendered a participant in natural life, followed by natural motions...

3. ...So the man who is reborn is rendered a participant in spiritual life through his rebirth from the Holy Spirit, followed likewise by spiritual motions.

4. Neither generation is devoid of life. Neither life is devoid of motion.

5. This inner renewal is often denoted with the phrase 'good works,' by way of synecdoche.

6. For renewal does not consist only in external good works or in passing actions, but also (and chiefly) in the inner renewal of the mind, of the will, and of all the powers of the soul.

7. From this inner newness flow good actions, and external good works testify to it.

8. Moreover, it has pleased the Holy Spirit to describe renewal with the phrase 'good works' for our sake, because external works are recognized more easily than the inner qualities of the soul and the dispositions of the heart.

9. In addition, all the praise of virtue consists in practice; we are renewed inwardly by the Holy Spirit so that the fruits of the Spirit may be visible outwardly.

10. Finally, in this way, hypocrisy is excluded, which is a feigned appearance of inner piety, which is only demonstrated in works that are also external.

11. As contrition, then, is the forerunner of the queen, [that is,] faith, so good works are the handmaidens.

12. For good works do not come before justification; they follow the one who has been justified (Augustine, *de fide et operibus, cap. 14.*).

13. And yet, where works do not appear on the outside, I will not believe that there is faith on the inside (John Huss).

14. Nor is it difficult to assign the cause of this perpetual connection between true faith and good works.

15. For it is the nature of true faith to be effective through love (Gal. 5:6).

16. He who believes is born of God (John 1:13). This certainly refers to the nature of his spiritual Father. But God is love (1 John 4:8). He who does not love does not know God.

17. Faith is the inner, salutary, and effective knowledge of God. How, then, could that highest Good, if He is truly known, not be loved? But if someone loves God, he will keep His word (John 14:23). He who has My commands and keeps them, says the Savior, he it is who loves Me (v. 21).

18. The apostle concludes from this, "In this we know that we have known Him, if we keep His commandments. Whoever says, 'I know Him,' and does not keep His commandments, is a liar, and the truth is not in him" (1 John 2:3–4).

19. Faith is the spiritual light from the soul, but where there is light on the inside, it sends forth its rays to the outside. Mat. 5:16: Let your light shine.

20. Christ dwells in hearts through faith (Eph. 3:17). Where Christ is, there is the Holy Spirit. Where the Holy Spirit is, there also the fruits of the Spirit appear.

21. Our faith is the victory which overcomes the world (1

John 5:4). But what is the world? It is the lust of the flesh, the lust of the eyes, and the pride of life (1 John 2:16). Where one securely indulges these, there the world has not yet been conquered, and therefore, true faith is not there.

22. Faith is living and victorious, if it is genuine.

23. Hearts are purified by faith (Acts 15:9). Therefore, where one securely indulges the impure filthiness of sin, can there be an inner purity of heart? From the abundance of the heart, the mouth speaks (Mat. 12:33).

24. These things had to be expressly explained in this way, not only in order that we might free ourselves from the Tridentine accusation—as if we preached with great contention that trust alone were removed from all duty—but also in order that the vain delusion of faith might be withdrawn from secure sinners.

25. To such people one must respond from James 2:26, that just as the body without the spirit, that is, without breath, is dead, so also faith without works is dead.

26. Not only do good works proceed from faith, but there are no truly good works except for those that proceed from faith.

27. Therefore, since faith keeps in view the Word as its correlative, the standard of good works is the divine Law, that is, the Decalogue.

28. Consequently, self-chosen forms of worship do not please God, but only those works which are done according to the rule of the moral Law contained in the Decalogue.

29. But the Decalogue must be understood according to the explanation of the prophets, Christ, and the apostles.

30. In addition, since faith does not arise from the natural powers of free will, but is a gift of the Holy Spirit, therefore, from what we have said—that works must proceed from faith—we further conclude that there are no truly good works except for the ones that are done by those who are born again through the Holy Spirit.

31. By nature, all men are dead in sins (Eph. 2:5; Col. 2:13).

32. Therefore, just as there is no spiritual life in those not yet reborn, so also there is no spiritual working that pleases God.

33. Thus Augustine rightly argues with great vigor that, without faith, the works that appear good are actually sins (*lib. 3. ad Bonifac. cap. 5.*, and in several other places).

34. Anselm argues that the entire life of unbelievers is sin, since there is nothing good without the highest Good (in *14. cap. Rom.*).

35. Those who say that this conclusion is cruel are truly the cruel ones (*Cens. Colon. pag. 29.*).

36. A bad tree cannot bear good fruits, and if a person is not yet reconciled to God, then the works of the person are not pleasing to God.

37. We can gather still more things from the proposition to be proved—that it is necessary for works that are truly good to proceed from faith. For from that it follows that, even if good works do not follow the perfection prescribed in the Law, nevertheless they are pleasing to God.

38. When Christ is apprehended by true faith, He renders both the man and his works, done by faith, acceptable to God.

39. Indeed, it should be understood in this sense, as is regularly said in our churches, that faith is the form of good works.

40. For we do not mean that the satisfaction of Christ is imputed to works in such a way that we are justified in the judgment of God through those works of ours.

41. For since the works themselves need to be justified (so to speak), they can by no means justify us.

42. But we say that those good works are pleasing to God for this very reason: because the person who has been reconciled through Christ works well by faith.

43. The good works of the reborn may be pleasing to God, but they do not placate God.

44. Finally, since good works proceed from faith, we are not justified before God through them or on account of them.

45. For that which we have already obtained through faith in Christ cannot be necessary in order for us to obtain it through works.

46. Therefore, when it is asked if we are justified and merit salvation by good works, the parameters of the question must be closely examined.

47. Good works are the works of the justified. Therefore, they are not justifying works (so to speak), just as good fruit, because it comes from a good tree, does not make the tree good.

48. We know that some try to answer by citing a distinction between a first and a second justification.

49. But this one thing more than any other example overturns that distinction: the apostle denies that Abraham, even in the course of doing good works, was justified before God by his works (Rom. 4:1–3). If anywhere, certainly in Abraham's case such a second justification by works—if it existed—would have taken place.

50. On the contrary, all the passages of Scripture that deny that we are justified by works overturn that distinction.

51. Good works are already owed to God. Therefore, we merit nothing by them (Luke 17:7).

52. Good works are imperfect and unclean, since renewal itself is not entirely complete in this life. How, then, can we merit eternal life by them? What are all the merits in the world in the face of such great glory? (Bernard, *serm. 1. in annunc. col. 106.*).

53. Good works are fruits of the Spirit, who drives and compels the reborn and works effectively in them. Therefore, man is more indebted to God on account of them, than deserving of something from God by them (Bernard, *ibid.*).

54. If good works could merit eternal life, then by all means they should and could also be done to that end, that we should gain

the reward of eternal life by them. But works done with this intention are not truly good works. For true love, although not without reward, does not seek a reward.

55. Thus far it has been preached concerning the subject of the question: to justify and to merit eternal life.

56. But if righteousness comes through Christ, then surely salvation does also. For he who has the Son has eternal life (John 3:39).

57. The nature of merit requires that the work by which we merit must be gratuitous, not something owed by us to the one for whom we do it. But whatever good we do is merely a part of our duty as a debt to God.

58. The nature of merit also requires that the work be useful and advantageous to the one from whom we are earning something. But God does not need our good deeds (Psalm 16:2).

59. Finally, the nature of merit requires that the thing offered by us must be of equal value and worth with the thing which we receive in its place. But there is a vast difference between the value of our works and the value of eternal life.

60. Eternal life is a free gift of God, and, therefore, not the merit of our works (Rom. 11:4).

61. Whatever you assign to merits is lacking in grace. I do not want any merit that excludes grace (Bernard, *sermon. 67. in Cant.*).

62. Surely we cannot merit even the crust of bread that we enjoy, but we are forced to beg God for it with daily prayers. How, then, can we merit eternal life?

63. Therefore, let another seek merit. For our part, let us be zealous to find grace (Bernard, *serm. in nativ. Mat. col. 213.*).

64. If those things which some people refer to as merits are properly named, they are, as it were, seedbeds of hope, incentives of love, proofs of a hidden predestination, prognostications of future happiness, the way of the kingdom, not the cause of the reigning (Bernard, *tract. de grat. et lib. arbitr.*, near the end.).

65. And yet, although good works are not necessary for meriting righteousness and salvation, nevertheless, they are necessary for the reborn: first, with respect to God, then, with respect to the neighbor, and, finally, with respect to the reborn themselves.

66. With respect to God, good works are necessary in many ways: (1) This is His will and commandment, that the reborn should do good. (2) He is the Father, we the children. Therefore, let us take after our Father. (3) For this purpose, we were created, (4) redeemed by Christ, (5) regenerated and sanctified by the Holy Spirit, that we should do good, (6) and that we may glorify God with our good works, (7) lest the most holy name and Word of God be heard poorly on account of us.

67. With respect to the neighbor, the necessity of doing good works compels us (1) to help him as a man by our duties; (2) to build others up by our good example; (3) to avoid offenses; (4) and to silence the mouth of wicked slanderers by doing good.

68. With respect to the reborn themselves, the zeal for doing good works compels them (1) to attest to the new creation in Christ by the newness of life; (2) to prove that they have been rescued from darkness by walking as children of light; (3) to produce true fruits of faith and, in this way, to make their calling sure; (4) to remove the suspicion of hypocrisy; (5) to avoid the temporal and eternal penalties appointed for evil works; (6) not to cast out faith, grieve the Holy Spirit, and lose the grace of God through sins; (7) to obtain bodily and spiritual rewards from God.

69. Faith is exercised in good works; it grows fat through them, as it were, and prospers (Dr. Luther in *cap. 17. Genes.*).

70. They must be encouraged and carefully inculcated, lest we think that the remission of sins and free justification gives us a special right to act shamefully.

71. Nevertheless, God receives us into grace out of free goodness for the sake of Christ, to the end that He may have a

people zealous for good works (Titus 2:14).

72. In verse 12, which comes just before this, the apostle establishes three classes, as it were, of good works. For he requires that we live σωφρόνως, δικαίως, καὶ εὐσεβῶς.

73. Εὐσέβεια has in view the forms of worship that are owed to God in the First Table, including the fear and love of God, trust in God, true invocation, confession, and thanksgiving.

74. Δικαιοπραγία has the neighbor in view, and includes all the duties of humanity that are owed to the neighbor, according to the standard of the Second Table, so that obedience and reverence are shown to one's superiors, counsel and aid to one's equals, protection and discipline to one's inferiors (Bernard, *serm. 3. de adv. Domini.*).

75. Σωφροσύνη has us in view and requires the discipline of the body as well as control of the emotions. No conquest is more glorious than the conquest of oneself.

76. In the same way, when the Savior, in opposition to the hypocritical Pharisees, wanted to point out the method of doing truly good works, He established three kinds of good works, as it were, namely, mercy, prayer, and fasting.

77. With the word 'mercy,' we understand by way of synecdoche the duties of love which are owed to the neighbor. From this comes the distinction explained in these verses between bodily and spiritual works of mercy. *I visit, I give to drink, I give to eat, I redeem, I cover, I harvest, I store up. Counsel, chastise, comfort, forgive, bear, pray.*

78. With the word 'prayer' is understood, also by way of synecdoche, all the devotion owed to God. For if prayer is to be pleasing to God, it must proceed from true faith in God, fear of God, and love for God.

79. With the word 'fasting' is understood the discipline of the body. For the flesh must be reared so that it obeys; it must be tamed so that it does not become proud, according to the saying of Hugo.

80. From all that has been said thus far, we assemble the following definition: Good works are actions commanded by God of men reborn, done out of faith in Christ, according to the standard of the divine Law, for the glory of God.

81. God grant that we be rich in such works, through Christ, the Author and Perfecter of faith and good works. May He be worshiped forever!

Chapter 16: The Sacraments

1. To the word of the Gospel, God has added the Sacraments, which are the visible Word...

2. And visible signs of invisible grace (Augustine, *lib. 19. cont. Faust. c. 16.*).

3. For through the Sacraments, that which is announced to the ears through the Word is, in a way, set before the eyes.

4. The word 'Sacrament' is, in fact, found in the Scriptures.

5. But not in the same sense in which it is used in this place.

6. And yet we should not, with Carlstadt, forbid the use of this word in the Church.

7. Indeed, it would be a miserable slavery to abstain entirely from the use of words not found in the Scriptures.

8. Among the secular writers, the word 'Sacrament' is used, first of all, for money deposited with the Pope by litigants, to the end that he who won a case in court might receive his whole deposit, while the deposit of the other man went to the papal purse.

9. Secondly, the word is used for that solemn oath by which soldiers used to be bound, with a certain rite and with prescribed words, to show loyalty to the republic and the magistrate.

10. From here, it later began to be transferred in general to any kind of oath.

11. In the Scriptures, the Latin translator uses 'Sacrament' for that which the Greeks call μυστήριον, which the Chaldeans called *Rasa*, and the Hebrews *Sod*.

12. The ecclesiastical writers understand a Sacrament to be a divinely instituted ceremony in which the good things promised in the Gospel are offered and applied to believers.

13. These Sacraments of ours are 'holy and unadulterated mysteries,' as Damascenus says (*4. orth. fide. cap. 14.*), or as (from the ancients) Jeremiah the Patriarch says (*Constant. resp. 1. ad Theol. Wirteb.*), φρικτὰ μυστήρια, 'horrible mysteries.' Certainly, then, the word 'Sacrament' was rightly attributed to them.

14. Through the Sacraments, we are bound to God for faith and obedience, just as soldiers are bound to the emperor with an oath. Through the Sacraments, we are also bound to one another for love, just as those who contended with one another in court were bound by their deposit of money to the pope.

15. Furthermore, while the word 'Sacrament' properly and very frequently is understood for the entire sacramental act, it is sometimes used improperly and by way of synecdoche to denote the other essential aspect of the Sacrament, namely, the external symbol, or, as Irenaeus says (*lib. 4. cap. 34.*), the earthly element.

16. Thus also the term 'Sacrament' sometimes denotes the salutary benefit of the Sacrament, and sometimes the other essential part of the Sacrament, namely, the heavenly element.

17. In addition, the Sacraments should be defined by actions. For wherever Sacraments are instituted, there certain actions are prescribed and required, nor is the essential integrity of the Sacraments intact unless those divinely prescribed actions are present.

18. Moreover, the actions are sacred and solemn because they were divinely instituted and because in them God deals with us and we with God.

19. It is God who not only originally instituted the Sacraments and commended them to the Church, but also still today dispenses the heavenly benefits through them by means of the ministry of man.

20. That sacramental dispensation consists in *giving* and *receiving*.

21. *Giving* refers to the divinely prescribed act of the one who administers the Sacrament. *Receiving* refers to the reception of it.

22. In both cases, one must distinguish between the matter itself and the manner of carrying it out. Giving and receiving are simply necessary. But the manner of giving and receiving allows for a certain degree of liberty.

23. We maintain that God alone has the power to institute the Sacraments.

24. For to institute the means of grace is the purview of Him whose purview it is to confer grace.

25. Therefore Thomas writes correctly (*p. 3. q. 64. art. 2.*): The power of the Sacrament comes from God alone. Therefore, God alone is the Institutor of the Sacraments.

26. Here He adds these noteworthy things: The apostles and their successors are the vicars of God with regard to the governing of the Church instituted by God through faith and through the Sacraments of faith. For this reason, just as they are not permitted to establish another Church, so also they are not permitted to teach another faith, nor to institute other Sacraments, but through the Sacraments which flowed from Christ's side as He was hanging on the cross, the Church of Christ is said to have been fashioned.

27. God also dispenses the Sacraments, yet not immediately, but ordinarily, through the ministers of the Church.

28. For they are the dispensers of the mysteries of God (1 Cor. 4:1) and God's coworkers (1 Cor. 3:9).

29. However, in extraordinary cases, in the Sacrament of initiation, when extreme necessity presses, the administration of it falls to other members of the Church.

30. Consequently, since the minister does this, not in his own name, but in the name of God, his worthiness or unworthiness can neither add to nor subtract from the efficacy of the Sacraments.

31. The life of the minister does not alter the power of the Sacrament.

32. The ministers here act instrumentally. However, an instrument acts, not according to its own form, but according to the power of him by whom it is moved (Thomas, *p. 3. q. 64. art. 5.*).

33. From here arise those illustrations of the ancients, that the life of the minister does not remove the benefit of the Sacrament, just as the light of the sun is not polluted by the dust and dirt through which it passes; just as it matters little for watering the garden whether the water flows through a channel made of stone or of silver; just as the shape of the wax seal remains the same, whether made by a ring of gold or of iron, etc. (Augustine, *tract. 5. in Joh. lib. 3. de Bapt. c. 10.* & Nazianzus, *orat. de Bapt.*).

34. We say the same thing concerning the intention of the minister; namely, that it is not required by absolute necessity for the integrity and fruit of the Sacrament.

35. For that non-intention (so to speak) is a species either of a minor blemish or of malice in the minister. Therefore, what is true of the genus is also true of the species.

36. Furthermore, the Sacraments were instituted only for men, and obviously, for the living. To them only, therefore, should the Sacraments be administered.

37. Two things are required for a Sacrament: the Word and the element.

38. The Word is added to the element and it becomes a Sacrament (Augustine, *de catacl. cap. 3. tract. 80. in Joh.*).

39. With 'the Word,' we understand, first, the divine institution through which the element, as it receives the call of God (as Irenaeus says in *lib. 4. cap. 34.*), is separated from common use and destined for sacramental use. Second, we understand the proper promise of the Gospel, which is to be applied and sealed through the Sacrament.

40. And consequently, with regard to each Sacrament, we should base our judgment on the divine institution, or, to say the same thing, on the proper *sedes* in which the divine institution is described.

41. And since each Sacrament has its peculiar institution, it also has its peculiar administration as the proper form.

42. And thus the substantive words of the institution of the Sacrament should by no means be altered.

43. There are two Sacraments in the Old Testament, and two in the New: Circumcision in the Old Testament, to which Baptism corresponds in the New; and the Paschal Lamb in the Old Testament, to which the Lord's Supper corresponds in the New.

44. If others are added to these, there is always something missing: either the divine institution, or the external element, or the proper promise of the Gospel.

45. There are several purposes of the Sacraments, but only two principal purposes; the rest are subordinate and lesser.

46. The first principal purpose is that the Sacraments are organs, means, and instruments through which God offers, distributes, and applies to believers the proper promise of the Gospel concerning the remission of sins, righteousness, and eternal life.

47. For anything that can be said of the Word must not be denied to the Sacraments, which are the visible Word; but the word of the Gospel is such an organ.

48. Through the Sacraments we are received into God's covenant and preserved in it. But it is a covenant of grace. Therefore, the Sacraments are surely organs of grace and salvation.

49. Therefore, we depart from those who detract from the Sacraments in their reception, turning them into bare signs which merely signify grace.

50. The fathers, to be sure, occasionally refer to the Sacraments as signs. But they understand them to be signs that seal[31], or, as the Augsburg Confession explains (art. 13), signs that testify of God's grace toward us.

---

31   *signa obsignantia*

51. In this sense, the apostle explains in Rom. 4:11 the word 'sign' (σημεῖον) used in Gen. 17:11 as a 'seal' (σφραγίς).

52. So also they sometimes call the external element of the Sacrament a sign, not merely signifying an absent, heavenly thing (for in this sense they expressly reject the words 'figure' and 'sign'), but distributing and offering the heavenly thing that is present and sacramentally united to the element.

53. For the sign is what it signifies and presupposes the invisibility—not the absence—of the thing signified.

54. The sign is the thing which, beyond the impression which it makes on the senses, causes something else to come to mind (Augustine, *2. de doct. Christ. c. 1.*).

55. Therefore, ignorantly and foolishly do some conclude from the word 'sign' the absence of the other essential part.

56. We also depart from those who excessively detract from the Sacraments and assert that they confer grace by the mere act of doing the work.

57. They explain it in this way: that good motives are not required in the recipient, that there is a certain supernatural power in the Sacraments by which they are the cause of grace just like fire is the cause of heat.

58. But just as the Word is of no benefit apart from faith (Heb. 4:2), so neither are the Sacraments, which are a visible Word.

59. Nor does it help for the benefit to be offered unless there is someone who receives it. The hands of God, the Giver, are Word and Sacraments. The hand of man, the recipient, is faith.

60. Hugo puts it beautifully (*5. de Sacram. p. 9. cap. 2.*): For the gift of grace—the spiritual things—like an antidote, are invisible. They are extended to man in the visible Sacraments as instruments. Just as that which is in a ladle is not made of the ladle, but is drawn out with it, so grace does not come from the Sacraments, nor is it made of the Sacraments, but arises from the eternal fountain.

From that fountain, grace is drawn by the soul in the Sacraments themselves.

61. And since we ascribe to the Sacraments this purpose in general, from that it can be concluded that we also attribute the same thing to the Sacraments of the Old Testament.

62. For the promise about reception into the covenant of grace had been added to circumcision, as described with these emphatic words: I will be your God and the God of your seed (Gen. 17:7). These words are to be explained from Lev. 26:12, Jer. 31:2, and Mat. 22:32, and it will be apparent that in them are contained the promise of God's grace, special indwelling, and eternal life.

63. Consequently, we also depart from those who argue that the Sacraments of the Old Testament were not instrumental causes of grace; that they did not possess any power from the suffering of Christ, etc.

64. The second chief purpose of the Sacraments is to be signs and seals of divine benevolence toward us, instituted for the purpose of strengthening faith in us.

65. For the apostle calls circumcision a 'seal of the righteousness of faith' (Rom. 4:11). But it is the nature of a seal to testify, to strengthen, and to seal that to which it is connected.

66. For this reason, the devout fathers drew effective comfort from circumcision in time of danger (1 Sam. 14:6; 17:26, 36).

67. Furthermore, what is said about the purpose of circumcision is also rightly applied to the rest of the Sacraments. Indeed, all the Sacraments meet together in the efficient cause and in the generic, final cause.

68. This is why Baptism is said to be the συνειδέσεως ἀγαθῆς εἰς θεὸν ἐπερώτημα. They use this word in the LXX when they say that the mouth of the Lord has been asked in the Old Testament. Oecumenius understands ἐπερώτημα as a pledge and a down payment.

69. Therefore, the sense is that Baptism testifies to our conscience and confirms it concerning the grace of God. Observe that the foundation of this seal is established in the resurrection of Christ, for He rose again for the sake of our righteousness (the result of which is peace of conscience) (Rom. 4:25, 5:1).

70. Here we also introduce the passage from 1 John 5:8: There are three who testify on earth: the Spirit, the water, and the blood. From the aim of the text of this passage and from the analogy of faith arises this paraphrase: that the Holy Spirit, in the ministry of the Gospel (which is the ministry of the Spirit [2 Cor. 3:8]), and the water in Baptism (which is the washing of water in the Word [Eph. 5:26]), and the blood (which is held out in the Lord's Supper to be drunk by us [1 Cor. 11:25]) testify to God's fatherly benevolence toward us.

71. From this, Tertullian (*lib. de poenit.*) calls Baptism a 'seal'[32] of faith. And Augustine (*de catech. rud. cap. 26.*) calls the Sacraments 'signs'[33].

72. Therefore, we depart from those who deny that the Sacraments are seals that seal the promise of grace.

73. Several secondary and lesser purposes of the Sacraments can be enumerated: They are the bonds of public gatherings. They are tokens by which the Church is distinguished from other assemblies. In them, we are bound to God for faith and obedience. They are types and likenesses of virtues, especially of love, etc.

74. The scholastics argue that a character is impressed on certain Sacraments.

75. They describe it in this way: that it is a spiritual sign impressed on the soul by God alone in the reception of an uniterable Sacrament, remaining indelibly according to common law.

76. Of the essence, subject, and purpose of this character,

---

32   *obsignationem*
33   *signacula*

we could enumerate the miserable and astonishing battles of the scholastics.

77. But we conclude with Biel (4. *sent. dist. q. 2.*): Neither does necessary reason demonstrate nor does clear authority prove that this character is to be assumed.

78. Indeed, all the authorities adduced from Dionysius, Augustine, Damascenus, and the Master (Lombard) are explained truly—and more pertinently to the thinking of those who propose such things—concerning the Sacrament or sacramental form of Baptism than concerning something that is actually impressed on the soul. Thus Biel.

79. The character of such things, then, is indeed indelible, because it is never written down in the first place.

80. These things have been said concerning the Sacraments in general, a definition of which is gathered from the things said above: The Sacraments are sacred and solemn acts, divinely instituted, in which God, through the ministry of man, dispenses a certain thing, instituted with a peculiar Word, to offer and to apply and seal to believers the proper promise of the Gospel.

81. May God, the only Author of the Sacraments, blessed forever, grant us to participate in them in a worthy and salutary manner.

Chapter 17: Holy Baptism

1. Baptism is the front door, the first gate of grace, the first entrance into the Church, the key of the kingdom of heaven, and the investiture of Christendom.

2. And, therefore, it is the first Sacrament of the New Testament, called 'the Sacrament of initiation' for that very reason.

3. The Greek word βαπτισμός denotes, generally, any kind of washing, that is, any manner of applying water, whether it is done by immersing or by pouring or by sprinkling.

4. Metaphorically, it is used in the Scriptures for the cross and troubles (Mat. 20:23); for the visible and abundant pouring out of the gifts of the Holy Spirit (Acts 1:5); for Israel's miraculous crossing of the Red Sea (1 Cor. 10:2).

5. By way of synecdoche, it is used for doctrine, and even for the whole ministry of John the first Baptizer (Mat. 21:5, etc.).

6. In its proper and preeminent usage, that is, as it is commonly used in the Church, the word is understood as that solemn mystery of initiation, namely, the first New Testament Sacrament.

7. Because of the one essential part, it is called 'water' in John 3:5, according to its essence; a 'washing of water in the word' in Eph. 5:26, according to its effect; a 'washing of regeneration and renewal of the Holy Spirit' in Titus 3:5, according to the type which came first; a 'circumcision not made with hands' (Col. 2:11).

8. The chief Author of Baptism, and therefore the ruling cause, is God.

9. For through the prophets He preached about this salutary washing, with types and prophecies even in the Old Testament.

10. The types are Noah's ark in the Flood (1 Pet. 3:20); circumcision (Col. 2:11); Israel's crossing of the Red Sea (1 Cor. 10:2); the water mixed with the blood of the sacrificed sparrow that was used to cleanse the lepers (Lev. 14:6); the water of expiation into which the ashes of the red heifer were scattered (Num. 19:20); various washings and sprinklings used among the Jews (Heb. 9:10); the water of the Jordan by which Naaman was cured of leprosy (2 Kings 5:14).

11. Some of the prophecies are presented with proper words, others with allegorical words. Psa. 29:10 – the Lord sits upon the flood. Psa. 46:5 – the streams of the river make glad the city. Isa. 49:22 – the Gentiles will bring your sons on their arms. Eze. 36:25 – I will sprinkle you with clean water and you will be cleansed from your impurities. Eze. 47:9 – the waters flowing from the temple make everything alive. Zec. 13:1 – On that day there will be a fountain opened to the house of David and to the inhabitants of Jerusalem in the washing away of sin and uncleanness. Joel 3:18 – a pure and salutary fountain will go forth from the house of the Lord and will water the scorched Sittim.

12. It is the same One who sent John in the New Testament to baptize, or to baptize with water (Luke 3:2, John 1:3), which is why the Baptism of John is said to be from heaven (Mat. 21:25) and the Pharisees who refused to be baptized by him are said to have despised the plan of God (Luke 7:30).

13. In a sense, Christ renewed this divine institution of Baptism after His death and resurrection with a solemn proclamation and mandate to spread it throughout the whole world.

14. Thus the Baptism of John was the same Sacrament as the Baptism of Christ, that is, the Baptism that Christ administered through the apostles, and that He still administers today through the ministers of the Church. It also had the same efficacy. Nor was it necessary, after John's Baptism, for a person to seek Baptism from Christ.

15. The same causes and the same effects prove the sacramental identity of both Baptisms.

16. Meanwhile, we do not deny that the visible pouring out of the wondrous gifts of the Holy Spirit were connected with the Baptism of the apostles, which were lacking in John's Baptism.

17. Moreover, God administers this Sacrament, not immediately, but through the ministers of the Church, to which it ordinarily pertains, as stewards of the mysteries of God (1 Cor. 4:1).

18. Since they, in turn, are ministers of a foreign good, their vices do not remove the essence or benefit of Baptism.

19. For this reason, even heretics, as long as they keep the essential elements of Baptism, administer a true Baptism.

20. We also maintain this position in the case when a minister of the Church privately and secretly holds to a heresy that runs contrary to the truth of Baptism, while the Church itself thinks differently.

21. But if any come to us having been baptized among the heretics in a non-Trinitarian invocation, we declare that they should be baptized, not rebaptized. For one should not believe that they have been baptized if water was not applied to them in the name of the Father, Son, and Holy Spirit.

22. We hold that in an extraordinary case of utmost necessity, it is also permissible for a private person to baptize.

23. For the order is of service to the Sacraments, but it does not govern them. Consequently, in a case of necessity it is permissible to act in an extraordinary way, as long as nothing is done contrary to the express Word of God.

24. We make no distinction here between men and women, since, in Christ, there is neither male nor female (Gal. 3:28).

25. The external element of Baptism is water; namely, natural and elemental water.

26. Therefore, as many as substitute some other liquid or some other external element, or who judge that such a substitution

can be made, depart from the divine institution.

27. Baptism is not simply water, but it is a washing of water in the Word (Eph. 5:26).

28. Therefore, neither the water without the Word, nor the Word without the water is reckoned a Baptism.

29. It is the word both of the command and of the promise.

30. For the apostles are commanded to baptize in the name of the Father and of the Son and of the Holy Spirit (Mat. 28:19). And the promise is added that, through Baptism, God wants to be effective in men for salvation (Mark 16:16).

31. Therefore, according to this word, the entire Holy Trinity—Father, Son, and Holy Spirit—is present in Baptism, just as the entire Trinity is present in the Baptism of Christ, who is the Head of the Church (Eph. 1:22).

32. The Father receives the baptized man into grace for the sake of the Son, the Mediator. The Son cleanses him from all sins by His own blood. The Holy Spirit regenerates and renews him for eternal life.

33. For if the entire Holy Trinity is present, then Christ the God-Man is certainly also present and with His blood cleanses the baptized person of the filth of his sins.

34. For this reason, the fathers say, and Dr. Luther repeats, that Baptism is made red with the blood of Christ (Augustine, *tract. 11. in Johan.*, Bede in *Psa. 80.*).

35. Therefore, the water of Baptism is not to be considered according to its natural properties and uses in common life. It should be viewed as a sanctified symbol and medium of the Word of God, with which and through which the entire Holy Trinity works in the baptized for their salvation.

36. The form of Baptism is that a man baptizes, that is, immerses or sprinkles with water, in the name of the Father, Son, and Holy Spirit.

37. And since the form represents the thing itself, if the form of Baptism is changed, then it is no longer a Sacrament.

38. Let the immersion or sprinkling be done three times or once; it does not affect at all the integrity of the Baptism. Let the usual rite of the Church be reverently observed in these matters of adiaphora.

39. The Trinity of Persons can be indicated with three immersions; the unity of the Divinity with one.

40. The words "in the name of the Father, of the Son, and of the Holy Spirit," are very emphatic and should be explained carefully and often to pious hearers.

41. For the minister professes that whatever he does in this act, he does not in his own name, but in the name and by the command of God.

42. He also shows that the true God, who is one in essence and three in Persons, is being invoked upon him who is being baptized.

43. Why, even the very words expressly testify that each Person of the most Holy Trinity is there in Baptism with His presence and efficacy of grace. The Father receives the baptized person into grace on account of the merit of the Son, and He seals him for salvation by the Holy Spirit.

44. For this reason, the baptized are called 'sons of God,' 'Christians,' and 'spiritual people,' because of the Father, the Son, and the Holy Spirit.

45. To this applies the dictum, 'creation and recreation, formation and reformation.' For as the Father created the first man, through the Son, in the Holy Spirit, so likewise in the Sacrament of regeneration, the entire Holy Trinity operates.

46. Finally, with these words the one who is baptized is bound to the name, that is, to the acknowledgement and invocation of this true God, so that he recognizes Him alone as the true God, calls upon Him, and serves Him throughout his whole life.

47. For it is necessary that you be baptized, as we have received, and that you believe, as we are baptized, and that you glorify, as we have believed, the Father and the Son and the Holy Spirit (Basil, *Epist.* 78.).

48. From this fountain flow all the praises that are found in the apostolic Scriptures concerning the salutary fruit of this mystery.

49. For example, that it is a washing of regeneration and renewal (Tit. 3:5); through which the Church is cleansed (Eph. 5:26); sins are washed away (Acts 22:16); Christ is put on (Gal. 3:27); and, in short, salvation takes place (1 Pet. 3:21).

50. For the sake of comparison, it is useful to consider the Baptism of Christ, who consecrated our Baptism. For that which is done there in visible symbols is done in our Baptism invisibly. But let us not doubt for a moment that it is truly done.

51. The Father receives us as sons on account of Christ. The Son washes us with His blood. The Holy Spirit regenerates and renews us and prepares in us a habitation for Himself. At last the door of Paradise is opened to us.

52. They depart from this simplicity and truth who deny that the water of Baptism, sanctified by the Word, is an efficacious medium through which the baptized person is regenerated and renewed.

53. On the contrary, they assert that the water of Baptism merely signifies and symbolizes what the Holy Spirit does inwardly in some people, and indeed at some future time.

54. What is more, they deny that the children of believers are baptized in order that they may first become children of God, since they are supposedly also in God's grace and in the covenant of grace before Baptism.

55. They say, moreover, that that adoption of which they are also participants before Baptism is merely sealed by Baptism.

56. Nor do they say that this is the office of Baptism in all

infants, but only in those who were elected to salvation by absolute decree.

57. Why, they expressly write that neither all children nor any children are actually regenerated in the moment of Baptism, but that the benefit of regeneration follows that act of Baptism in infants at its divinely-appointed, later time, from the Word that is heard.

58. How can all these things finally be reconciled with those distinguished praises which are attributed by the apostles to this salutary washing?

59. Surely in this way no saying of Scripture that deals with the fruit of Baptism can ever be explained properly and in a literal sense. By this sacramental analogy—which is not drawn from the Scriptures but imposed on them—all things are transformed into a foreign understanding.

60. But we, clinging to a literal sense of the words (which, as we have shown in its place, should always be done in the articles of faith), firmly believe that Baptism is an effective medium by which a man is regenerated and renewed to eternal life.

61. This purpose embraces within itself adoption, the remission of sins, ingrafting into Christ, sanctification, and the inheritance of eternal life.

62. But we deny that Baptism impresses an indelible character; or that it confers grace by the mere act of doing the work; or that it removes and utterly erases everything that has to do with guilt and punishment; for about all these things the Scriptures are silent.

63. Furthermore, since God, in Baptism, enters into a covenant of grace with man, its efficacy most certainly endures throughout a person's entire life.

64. For the covenant of God is not rendered void on account of our unbelief (Rom. 3:3).

65. Therefore, even if we, on our part, depart from that covenant, nevertheless the way back to it lies open to us through true and genuine conversion.

66. We learn to whom this Sacrament pertains from the divine institution, in which all nations are commanded to be baptized.

67. And yet it is to be done in the order and in the manner which Christ there prescribes, that those who are able, according to their age, to hear the Gospel should first be taught and then baptized.

68. Therefore, since all men are either children or adults, one must deal with each group distinctly.

69. Those infants are to be baptized who are either born of Christian parents (it makes no difference whether both are Christians or whether only one of them is), or who are given over to their guardianship.

70. Therefore, illegitimate children and foundlings whose Baptism is in doubt are not excluded here, nor are those who were born with some external defect, etc.

71. However, those infants who are not yet born are excluded, for no one can be born again unless he has first been born. Likewise the children of unbelievers are excluded, as long as they remain in their power.

72. Those adults are to be baptized who profess the Christian religion after they have been instructed about Christ.

73. Nor are women excluded here, as the apostolic practice (besides other arguments) confirms (Acts 8:12, 16:15).

74. Many things serve to confirm this position of ours from the Scriptures concerning infant baptism, but it will be useful to consider the following hypotheses:

75. First, infants are conceived and born in sin, and, therefore, are children of wrath by nature.

76. Secondly, God also wants children to be brought to Him, for it is not His will that one of these little ones should perish.

77. Thirdly, one cannot deal with them through the preaching of the Word. Therefore, there remains only one means, namely, Baptism, which has taken the place of circumcision.

78. Beware making the claim that 'Baptism is useless for infants, since they do not believe, nor can they believe.'

79. For in Baptism and through Baptism the Holy Spirit kindles faith in infants, so that, no less than circumcision, it is for them a seal of the righteousness of faith (Rom. 4:11).

80. Although we cannot understand how the faith of infants is acquired, nevertheless we should not on that account deny the working of the Holy Spirit.

81. If you ask about the infants who die without Baptism, you must proceed by making a distinction.

82. Those who are outside of the Church are left to the judgment of God.

83. But let those who are born of Christian parents and, excluded from Baptism by some great case of necessity, could not be baptized, or whose mother's womb became their grave, be commended to God with the pious prayers of their parents and of the Church. They are not excluded from the fellowship of the heavenly kingdom.

84. It remains for us to deal with certain circumstances which are normally observed in the administration of Baptism.

85. Wicked and superstitious ceremonies are to be rejected.

86. But those rites which, by their nature as adiaphora, lying in the middle, are not opposed to the analogy of faith, but rather are commended by apostolic authority and the early Church, and which, in addition, render the action, benefit, and efficacy—indeed, the necessity and dignity—of Baptism more perceptible to the less educated, are not simply and with offense to the Church to be rejected.

87. Exorcism is to be explained in this way: It is a testimony of the spiritual captivity of infants in the kingdom of the devil; of

the power and efficacy of Baptism by which the infants are transferred from the kingdom of Satan into the kingdom of Christ; and of the goal of the ecclesiastical ministry, which, in addition to the application of the benefits of Christ, consists in the perpetual struggle against Satan.

88. But the Church has the freedom to set forth and explain its doctrine of original sin, of the power and kingdom of Satan, and of the efficacy of Baptism with other words that are more in harmony with the Scripture (Dr. Chemnitz, *part. 3. Locor. Theolog.* p. 178.).

89. It is a very ancient custom to employ sponsors, that is, guarantors whom they call godfathers and godmothers, whose duty it is (1) to pray for the children, that God would receive them into grace through Baptism; (2) to repeat this very thing in their response, which Christ, as the mouth of the children, has testified on their behalf; (3) to instruct them in the chief matters of piety if their parents die.

90. It is entirely appropriate that a child be named in Baptism, not only because it was done long ago in circumcision, but especially in order to teach that in Baptism our names are written in the Book of Life (Luke 10:20, Rev. 20:15), and that our name is added to the register of Christian soldiers, so that we may fight from now on under the banners of Christ.

91. More has been written elsewhere concerning other ceremonies and circumstances. Here we shall only add that it is desirable that Baptism be administered at a larger gathering of the Church, during the morning service, and thus the administration of this most hallowed mystery be carried out with greater attention and devotion.

92. And yet, we do not maintain that one should depart rashly and by private initiative from the custom of each Church, nor do we prescribe laws in the case of necessity.

93. From all these things we deduce that Baptism is the first Sacrament of the New Testament in which a living person is submerged in water, or otherwise washed with it, in the name of the Father, of the Son, and of the Holy Spirit, so that, regenerated and renewed, he becomes an heir of eternal life.

94. May God, who has received us into His covenant of grace through Baptism, preserve us in it unto the end.

Chapter 18: The Holy Supper

1. The second Sacrament of the New Testament is the Lord's Supper, so called from its Author and from the time of its institution (1 Cor. 11:20).

2. It is also called 'the Lord's Table,' to distinguish it from profane feasts (1 Cor. 10:20); 'the Communion of the body and blood of Christ,' in which the essence of this Sacrament consists (1 Cor. 10:16); 'the Testament of Christ,' since in it all the requirements of a Testament appear (Luke 22:20, 1 Cor. 11:26); 'the breaking of bread,' since the Eucharistic bread used to be prepared in this way for distribution (Acts 2:42, 26, 20:7).

3. The ancients call it 'the Eucharist,' from 1 Cor. 11:26, since solemn thanks are to be given to Christ in the use of this Sacrament; they call it 'the Synaxis,' from 1 Cor. 11:20, since this holy Supper used to be celebrated in the public gathering of the Church and is a symbol of a mutual bond in Christ; they call it 'agape' on account of the sacred feasts instituted from the offerings collected for common use, 1 Cor. 11:21; they call it 'leitourgia,' because it is not an insignificant part of the public ministry.

4. We think that the word 'Mass' was derived from the formula of dismissal used by the fathers, in which they used to say to the catechumens, to those possessed by devils, and to those who had been excommunicated, *Ite, missa est* (B. Rhenanus *super 4. lib. Tertull. adv. Marc.*).

5. Various and diverse types of this Sacrament can be enumerated from the Old Testament. But the better ones are the Paschal Lamb (Exo. 12:47 ff., 1 Cor. 5:7); and manna, that bread of angels (Exo. 16:15, Psa. 78:26, John 6:49–50, 1 Cor. 10:3–4).

6. The Author of this Sacrament who instituted it and commended it to the Church is Christ (Mat. 26:26, Mark 14:22, Luke 22:19, 1 Cor. 11:23)…

7. Who is true God and one God with the Father and the Holy Spirit, omnipotent, true, all-wise, our Mediator and Savior. Therefore, if we wish to be His true disciples and listen, we should put faith in His words without any hesitation and rest in them (John 8:31).

8. It is the same Christ who, still today, in the distribution of the Eucharistic bread and wine, holds out His body and blood through the hands of the minister to be eaten and drunk.

9. Believe, therefore, all of you! For even now, that Supper is celebrated at which Christ once reclined. There is no difference between that one and this, for this celebration is not done by man, while that one was done by Christ. Do not think that it is the priest's hand stretched out to you. Know that it is the hand of Christ (Chrysostom, *hom. 51. in cap. 24. Matth.*).

10. Not that He administers this Supper today immediately, as He originally instituted it immediately, but He has been pleased to use the work of the Church's ministers for this. They are the stewards of the mysteries of God (1 Cor. 4:1).

11. The Eucharist consists of two things: an earthly thing, namely, bread and wine; and a heavenly thing, namely, the body and blood of the Lord (Irenaeus, *lib. 4. cap. 34.*).

12. One thing is seen, which the eyes also attest—that there is bread and the cup. The other thing faith needs to be taught—that the bread is the body of Christ, that the cup is the blood of Christ. These things are called Sacraments because in them one thing is seen, while the other thing is understood. That which is seen has a bodily appearance. That which is understood has a spiritual fruit (Augustine, *serm. ad Neoph.*, Beda in *1 Cor. 10.*).

13. Therefore, since bread and wine have been established for this Sacrament by the express ordination of Christ, neither of

these elements should be exchanged for something analogous.

14. Nothing here is holier or better or safer than that we be content with the authority of the one Christ.

15. Beyond that, it matters not for the integrity of the Sacrament whether the loaf is large or small, oblong or round; or whether the wine is red or white, since none of these things departs from the institution of Christ.

16. But we do strongly approve the Nicaean Canon that we should not consume much, but little, so that we recognize that it is not being consumed to fill our bellies, but for our sanctification.

17. In the same way, we do not think that it matters whether the bread is leavened or unleavened. Nor do we approve the battle over bread which was stirred up long ago among the Greeks and Latins.

18. Nevertheless, we use unleavened bread, according to the custom of the Church, on account of the example of Christ and the reminders which unleavened bread provides, which are not to be despised.

19. We affirm that the Eucharistic wine need not be mixed with water, since express mention is made only of the fruit of the vine (Mat. 26:29).

20. But we do affirm that it is necessary for all who approach this venerable Sacrament to be given not only bread, but also wine.

21. Either they should receive the Sacraments whole, or they should be prevented from receiving the whole thing, for the division of one and the same mystery cannot be done without great sacrilege, as we find in *dist. 2. de consecr.*

22. The eating is instituted separately from the drinking by that wisdom to which all human wisdom should yield concerning the inseparability of the living blood from the living flesh. For here one should not argue based on human reason, but the will of Christ

should be kept in view, who did not institute a crippled banquet, but added drink to the food (Andr. Fric. *4. de Reip. emend. c. 19.*).

23. What Christ has joined together, let not man ever separate (Mat. 19:6).

24. We do not disapprove seeking certain analogies between the bread and the body of Christ, between the wine and the blood of Christ, as long as one does not pretend that the whole Sacramental office of Eucharistic bread and wine depends on it.

25. Because, of course, it consists in this, that the Eucharistic bread is the communion of the body of Christ, and the cup which we bless is the communion of the blood of Christ (1 Cor. 10:16).

26. We firmly believe in this true, real, and substantial presence of the body and blood of Christ in the Supper, in adherence to the words of Christ, who declares that that which is given to be eaten in the Holy Supper is His body, who asserts that that which is given to be drunk in the Supper is His blood (Mat. 26:26–27; Mark 14:22–24; Luke 22:19–20; 1 Cor. 11:24–25).

27. It is not safe to recoil from these words of the Lord's Testament, faithfully handed down to us in the unwavering description of the three Evangelists and in the Pauline repetition, for the word which Christ has spoken will judge us on the Last Day (John 12:48).

28. The heavenly wisdom in the words of the Supper stops up all the cracks formed by such figurative interpretations through which the absence of the body and blood of Christ is introduced.

29. For Christ declares that He is giving His body—the very body that was given into death for us—to be eaten; and His blood—the very blood that was shed for our sins on the altar of the cross—to be drunk.

30. Therefore, in this matter we hold strictly to the literal sense of the words, just as we do in all the other passages in which the articles of faith are presented as in their proper *sedes*.

31. This brings about lasting peace to the conscience, for

the conscience finds no place to rest when it departs from the words of Christ and seeks a foreign understanding from other passages.

32. Nor should anyone here set against us the truth of the human nature in Christ and of His ascension into heaven, for we embrace those articles with the immovable certainty of faith, just as we embrace this article of the true presence of the body and blood of Christ in the Supper.

33. We give Christ this honor, that, by the power of His promise, He is able to give us His body and blood in the Supper while leaving intact the integrity of His human nature, although how He does or is able to do this, we are not able to discover.

34. Surely He can do more than we understand (Eph. 3:20). We enjoin this pronouncement of the Holy Spirit to repose in our inmost senses.

35. For from this it is clearly deduced that the judgment concerning the true contradiction in articles of faith is not to be commended to human reason.

36. In addition, the legitimate and Scripturally harmonious explanation of those articles concerning the personal union of the assumed nature with the Logos and of the ascension of Christ into heaven, followed immediately by His session at the right hand of God, clearly affirms that power by which Christ can do that which He has promised—so far from being the case that what He says about the Supper should falter.

37. For none of us proposes or even imagines a local inclusion of Christ's body in the bread and of His blood in the wine; or impanation; or the incorporation in the bread; or a physical non-existence; or of a hidden particle of His body under the bread; or a penetration of two bodies; or a Capernaitic cannibalism.

38. All these things are dreams of human reason as it seeks to inquire the mode of the sacramental presence—dreams which arise, for the most part, from a desire to slander.

39. We say with the apostle that the Eucharistic bread is the communion of the body of Christ, that the Eucharistic wine is the communion of the blood of Christ. We deny that the mode of this communion can be discovered.

40. Therefore, let glory be given to the words of Christ, and let sad contentions finally come to an end.

41. The form of this Sacrament consists in the blessing of bread and wine; the distribution of the blessed bread and wine; the eating and drinking of the bread and wine.

42. The sacramental blessing does not consist in some sort of magical conversion of the bread into the body of Christ and of the wine into the blood of Christ through a secret power lying in those words.

43. It is the sacred and efficacious designation of the external elements for sacramental use. For this reason, it is called 'consecration.'

44. Therefore, when the minister of the Church, following the institution of Christ and the example of the apostles (of which Gregory, *lib. 7. cap. 63. in Registro*, Platina, in *vita Xysti primi*, and many others write), repeats the words of institution, and precedes them with the Lord's Prayer, let us not at all conclude that this is a merely historical reading of the text.

45. No, first the minister testifies that he is not acting here, nor does he wish to act, by his own will, but that, as a legitimate steward of the mysteries of God, he is performing this sacred and solemn act in the name of Christ.

46. Then, presenting the bread and wine in this way, he sets them aside for sacred use, so that they are no longer merely conveyors of bread and wine, but of the body and blood of Christ.

47. Thirdly, he prays earnestly that Christ, being mindful of His promise, would be present in this sacramental action, and that He would distribute His body and blood together with these external symbols.

48. Finally, He testifies that, by the power of the Lord's institution and promise, the Eucharistic bread is the communion of the body of Christ, and the cup of blessing is the communion of the blood of Christ, and he admonishes all who are about to approach to remember that they are guests of Christ, to rely on His words with true faith, and to be genuinely concerned with preparing themselves to use the Sacrament in a salutary manner.

49. Furthermore, the Scripture not only nowhere says, but even contradicts the teaching that, through the consecration or blessing, the bread is converted into the body of Christ, or the wine into the blood of Christ.

50. This teaching of transubstantiation is strengthened very little, either in name or in substance, by the arguments of the more recent authors who explain it in this way: that the body of Christ is made from the bread, not as from the material, as He was made from the flesh of the Virgin Mary, but as from the *terminus a quo*, as heaven was made from nothing, as night is made from day, and as wine is made from water.

51. For besides the fact that they are departing from the view of their predecessors (who assert the essential conversion of bread and wine into the body and blood of Christ), they are also tangling themselves up in very great difficulties.

52. For if someone says that one substance is converted into another when it takes the place of it, he is abusing the terms.

53. Who ever said that nothing was transubstantiated into heaven, or that day is transubstantiated into night?

54. But if the body of Christ is made of bread in this way, as wine is made of water, it follows that the essence of bread is converted into the body of Christ; the accidents of bread vanish; those who hold Mass change the bread into the body of Christ by the same power with which Christ changed water into wine; and thus they are the creators of the Creator Himself, as the *Stella Clericorum* says.

55. Christ meant to institute a Sacrament, not a new creation; He meant to institute the communion of His body and blood through those external elements, not the transubstantiation of those elements into a heavenly substance.

56. And that it may be clear how this transubstantiation has absolutely no basis in the words of Christ, "This is My body; this is My blood," we will leave out the other things and hear only what Biel, the anthologist of Scholastic Theology, has to say in this matter.

57. This is what he says in *lib. 4. sentient. dist. 11. q. 1. art. 3. dub.*: (1) All affirmative propositions, in which the terms signifying the bread and the body of Christ are both placed in the nominative case, are false. 'The bread is the body of Christ. What the bread is, is, was, will be or can be the body of Christ' (he argues from the hypothesis of transubstantiation). The propositions are true in which the *terminus a quo*, that is, the bread and wine, is expressed with the ablative with the preposition *ex* or *de*, or the *terminus ad quem*, that is, the body and blood of Christ, is expressed with the accusative with the preposition *in*. Therefore, the following propositions are true: 'The body of Christ is made from bread, the blood of Christ is made of wine.' These are also true: 'The bread crosses over, is converted, or transubstantiated into the body of Christ.' Thus far Biel.

58. Therefore, the entire structure which they build as a tower to support transubstantiation topples to the ground, for Christ never said, 'My body is made from this bread, My blood is made of this wine.'

59. The superstructure surrounding transubstantiation is the practice of reserving, carrying around, and worshiping the external elements. Therefore, the same judgment applies to these.

60. The other sacramental act is the distribution, to which the breaking is attached.

61. Therefore, it matters not whether the breaking takes place before or after the blessing, as long as the distribution is added.

62. For the breaking does not constitute a peculiar sacramental act, but is a preparatory ministerial act.

63. Whether the external elements are placed in the mouth or in the hand of the communicants, it neither adds to the integrity of the Sacrament nor detracts from it.

64. For the substance and the mode of delivering the substance must be distinguished.

65. Those who argue that the breaking is a peculiar sacramental act representative of the Lord's Passion translate this into an action which is entirely different from that which was instituted by Christ.

66. For, based on the institution, the bread of Christ is the means and instrument through which Christ distributes His body. But they say that it is a sign which signifies the body of Christ, just as the breaking of the bread signifies the crucifixion.

67. If, then, they introduce clear and perspicuous foundations of their opinion from the words of institution, let them also show that a true and properly called 'breaking' in Christ's body is represented by this breaking of bread.

68. Indeed, let them also demonstrate the same representation in the other part of the Holy Supper, or let them stop disturbing the Churches on account of a rite that is, by its nature, an adiaphoron.

69. The third sacramental action is the eating and drinking, which does not have in view bread alone, that is, by itself, and wine alone, that is, by itself, but that bread which is the communion of the body of Christ, and that wine which is the communion of the blood of Christ (1 Cor. 10:16).

70. That eating is neither merely natural nor merely spiritual. Instead, it is a sacramental eating, dependent on the sacramental union of the bread and the body of Christ.

71. Therefore, as a sacramental union through which, in the true and legitimate use, the body of Christ is united with the bread, the blood of Christ with the wine, so also the sacramental eating (and drinking) depends on the institution of the truthful and omnipotent Christ. But this can be neither comprehended nor investigated by human reason.

72. Therefore, if one wishes to contrast a spiritual eating with a natural, carnal, physical, local, and Capernaitic eating, then we rightly assert that the eating of the body of Christ with the bread is spiritual.

73. But if, by 'spiritual eating,' one understands that which is treated in John 6, then that pertains to the fruit of the Supper, and, therefore, not at all to its essence.

74. The purpose of the Holy Supper is set forth in the words of Christ, "Do this in remembrance of Me."

75. This remembrance has in view the preceding words, that the body which was given into death for us is being eaten, and the blood which was poured out for our sins on the altar of the cross is being drunk.

76. From this, it is clear that the primary and principal purpose of the Holy Supper is the strengthening of faith.

77. This remembrance also includes within itself these fruits: that in the true and salutary use of the Lord's Supper, the promise of the remission of sins is sealed, the grace received in Baptism is confirmed, the friendly covenant between God and man is restored, spiritual gifts are increased, the ingrafting into Christ is renewed, and, finally, the believer feeds on incorruptible food for eternal life.

78. Briefly, when these things are taken and drunk, they cause Christ to remain in us, and us in Him (Hilary, 8. *de Trin.*).

79. Ignatius: "The Eucharistic bread is a medicine of immortality, the antidote to prevent us from dying." Basil: "The traveling provisions of eternal life, an acceptable defense against the fear-

ful utterance of God." Damascenus: "The deposit of the future life and kingdom."

80. Several lesser purposes can be enumerated: By the use of this Sacrament we confirm obedience to God, a beneficial memorial that is pleasing to Christ, our repentance to men, our consensus in doctrine, and genuine zeal for love.

81. But we completely deny that this mystery is either a propitiatory sacrifice or a sacrifice for obtaining grace.

82. For there is only one Priest of the New Testament, one propitiatory sacrifice, one offering.

83. No one should be admitted to the use of the Holy Supper except for Christians, and only those Christians who can examine themselves (1 Cor. 11:28).

84. Therefore, we know what decision is to be made concerning notorious sinners who refuse to examine themselves, and concerning children and others who cannot examine themselves.

85. True examination consists in the genuine recognition and hatred of sins, true faith in Christ, and the serious determination to amend one's life.

86. True faith in Christ also involves professing the real presence of Christ's body and blood in the Supper.

87. The unworthy eat and drink judgment on themselves because they do not discern the body of Christ (1 Cor. 11:29).

88. For since they eat unworthily of this bread (which is the communion of the body of Christ) and drink unworthily of this cup (which is the communion of the blood of Christ), they are therefore guilty of the body and blood of Christ (1 Cor. 11:27).

89. For the integrity of the Sacrament, therefore, it matters not with what faith a person approaches; but it matters immensely for the salutary benefit of it (Augustine, 3. *contra Donat. c. 14*.).

90. If asked about the time, place, and the other circumstances surrounding the Holy Supper, we answer with that apos-

tolic declaration, "Let all things be done decently and in order" (1 Cor. 14:40).

91. God will one day raise our bodies from their graves unto life, for they have been nourished with the body and blood of Christ (Irenaeus, *lib. 4. adv. haer. cap. 34.*).

Chapter 19: The Church

1. The Church on earth is gathered to God as the Holy Spirit effectively works through the Word and Sacraments.

2. The Church is so called because it is called out of the human race and gathered into a holy assembly.

3. For the Church is the assembly of men who have been gathered to the kingdom of God by the ministry of the Word and Sacraments. In this assembly, there are always some truly godly people who persevere in the true faith until the end, mixed together with many who are not saints, even though, by profession, they agree with the doctrine.

4. This assembly, since it must continually fight under the banner of Christ against the devil, the world, and the flesh, is called the 'Church Militant.'

5. And since the ministry of teaching the Word and administering the Sacraments falls upon the senses, the same assembly is for that reason called a 'Visible Church.'

6. But since it is not evident to the eyes of men which ones in that assembly are truly believing and godly, therefore it is called, with respect to them, an 'Invisible Church.'

7. Hence that distinction between a Visible and Invisible Church does not introduce two distinct Churches, as if they were different assemblies.

8. But it considers the assembly of the called from two different perspectives; namely, from the outside and from the inside.

9. The inner splendor of the Church consists in faith and renewal, with which the inheritance of eternal life is immediately combined.

10. The former spiritual regeneration and renewal in this life is covered, as with a veil, in weaknesses of the flesh. The latter communion of eternal life is covered in the offense of the cross and death, and for this reason the Church is said to be invisible.

11. The external splendor of the Church consists in the pure preaching (and profession) of the Word and the legitimate administration of the Sacraments, in which respect the Church is said to be visible.

12. Therefore, in order for a person to be a true and living member of this mystical body of Christ, that external profession of the same doctrine and the participation in the same Sacraments is not enough, but must be accompanied by the inner regeneration and indwelling of the Holy Spirit.

13. Nevertheless, the Invisible Church is not to be sought outside the Visible Church, but is included in it, since the elect are not to be sought outside the assembly of the called.

14. Nor is that Invisible Church of elect people to be sought anywhere in a pure and segregated state, externally isolated from all hypocrites.

15. For here (in this life) the Jebusite dwells among the inhabitants of Jerusalem; here in the garden of the Father of the household there are at once wild plants and fir trees, stinging-nettles and myrtles; in the flock of Jacob are white animals and black, sheep and goats; in Peter's net there are good fish and bad; in the field of the Lord there are lilies among the thorns; on the Lord's threshing floor there is wheat with chaff; in Christ's cellar there is wine with unripe fruit, oil with amurca; in Noah's ark there are clean animals and unclean.

16. This assembly, this Church, is adorned by the Holy Spirit with the most beautiful and honorable praises in Scripture.

17. For it is called 'the Body of Christ,' 'the Bride of Christ,' 'the kingdom of God,' 'the possession of God,' 'the beloved people,' etc.

18. But all these designations are synecdochal. For those praises are attributed to the Church on account of the truly reborn and elect who are in that assembly.

19. For it is clear that there is and remains a distinction between the truly reborn and the hypocrites who are joined to the Church only by outward profession.

20. The former are the true and living members of the Church, for they draw Spirit and life from Christ as the Head; the latter are rotten and dead members. The former belong to the Church internally, the latter externally; the former in the heart, the latter in external appearance; the former truly, the latter fictionally; the former by the judgment of God, the latter only by the judgment of men; the former as true and healthy parts of the body, the latter as mange and toxic fluids; the former are of the Church, properly speaking, the latter are only in the Church (Augustine *in brevic. collat., collat. 3. in Johan., tract. 6. de Bapt. lib. 3. cap. 18.*, etc.).

21. In the Apostles' Creed the Church is said to be 'one, holy, catholic and apostolic.'

22. It is said to be 'one' on account of the unity of the Spirit, which the apostle explains in Eph. 4:3ff.: "There is one body and one Spirit, just as you were also called into one hope of your calling. One Lord, one faith, one Baptism, one God and Father of all, who is over all and through all and in you all."

23. It is said to be 'holy,' because it is sanctified by Christ through the Spirit and the Word. In this life, such holiness consists in the imputation of the holiness of Christ and in zeal for true holiness. But in the future life, that holiness will finally be perfected.

24. It is said to be 'catholic' with respect to the catholic faith, which is to be reckoned from the common consensus of all the pious, at whatever time and in whatever place they lived or still live, in the true doctrine.

25. But it is altogether necessary that such consensus rest on the catholic writings of the prophets and apostles, which are the only foundation of the Church (Eph. 2:20).

26. It is said to be 'apostolic,' because it began to be propagated in the New Testament by the apostles (who taught nothing apart from Moses and the prophets [Acts 26:22]), and it is still today being gathered by means of the their doctrine as it is expressed in the Scriptures.

27. From these things it can easily be deduced what the true signs of the true Church are; namely, the pure preaching of the Word and the legitimate administration of the Sacraments.

28. For since the Church is nothing other than the assembly of those who publicly profess the true doctrine of Christ and who legitimately use the Sacraments—and indeed there is no surer mark of a thing than its form—we conclude that there are no other genuine and proper marks of the Church.

29. If any other marks are assigned, namely, the name 'Catholic,' antiquity, duration, size, succession of bishops, temporal prosperity, etc., these the Church holds in common with other assemblies, nor do they have any importance except for when they coincide exactly with those other marks of ours.

30. Concerning this matter we note the words of Stapleton in *relect. princ. fidei controv. 1. quest. 4. art. 5. p. 113*. As people discern a man from a beast—children do so by the outline of the body and the form of a man, since the evidence of these things does not go beyond the senses; adults, having also the use of reason, though unlearned and coarse, do so by the deeds of life and by the functions that are characteristically human, such as speaking in the manner of men, walking, and similar things; the wise and the learned, whose judgment enters more deeply, do so by the learning of the mind and by the other talents that are still more excellently characteristic to man—

31. So the Church is recognized, by the wise and the spiritual, of which sort are the teachers and pastors of the Church, through sound doctrine and the right use of the Sacraments; by the inexperienced believers and children in the faith, who are unable to make a judgment regarding the doctrine itself as considered in its basic causes and means; and also by the unbelievers themselves, who know little or nothing about the Church, through the external appearance and multitude of believing people and pastors.

32. We insist that this comparison of Stapleton be noted carefully. For from it we can conclude that our marks are proper, genuine, and well-suited for spiritual men, while their marks are dubious and uncertain.

33. We gladly concede to them the external form of the Church with its outline. Let them leave the soul to us.

34. To the same pertains what Bellarmine expressly admits: that by those marks, which he himself has assigned, it is not rendered manifestly true that the Roman Church is the true Church of God, but it is, nevertheless, rendered manifestly credible (*Lib. 4. de Eccles. c. 3. col. 210.*).

35. Furthermore, since the preaching of the Gospel and the administration of the Sacraments is not done in all particular churches with equal purity, but the leaven of human traditions and opinions is mixed in by some people with the pure lump of the divine Word, therefore, in this respect and in this sense, the Church is said to be more or less pure.

36. Thus Christ commands that the scribes and Pharisees, who sit in Moses' seat, be heard (Mat. 23:2), that is, as those who set forth the doctrine handed down by Moses, as Biel interprets (*4. sent. dist. 1. q. 4. art. 3*). At the same time, however, He also commands to beware of their leaven, that is, of their false doctrine (Mat. 16:6).

37. God is able to produce spiritual children for Himself, even through a corrupt ministry (Eze. 16:20).

38. The ears of the students are often purer than the lips of the teachers.

39. Thus the papacy is not the true and pure Church. At the same time, however, God did gather the Church to Himself in former times under the papacy, and still today gathers it to Himself in the midst of Rome.

40. Our Churches have left the Roman Babylon, in accord with the divine command (Jer. 15:19). They have separated the precious from the vile. They have accepted and still profess the prophetic and apostolic Scriptures and the doctrine that conforms to them, segregated from the leaven of human traditions.

41. Therefore, is there anyone who can deny the apostolic name to our Church? As the doctrine is, so is the Church. The apostolic doctrine produces an apostolic Church.

42. Therefore, either let them convince us from the prophetic and apostolic Scriptures that we have seceded from the doctrine of the prophets and apostles, or let them surrender to us the name of the catholic and apostolic Church.

43. Here we insist that one take careful note of what the acts of the Assembly of Augsburg testify in the year 1530, that the chief men from among our adversaries at that time confessed that they were unable to refute the confession of our faith from the Scriptures.

44. Therefore, we submit from Augustine's *Epist.* 166.: "In the Scriptures we have come to know Christ; in the Scriptures we have come to know the Church. How do we not, in the Scriptures, retain both Christ and the Church in common?"

45. We would also remind them of what Augustine wrote *de unit. Eccles. c.* 2.: "Between us and the Donatists (the Romanists), the question is, where is the Church? What, then, shall we do? Shall we seek the Church in our words, or in the words of our Lord, who is the Church's Head? I think that we should seek it in the words of Him who is the truth and who knows His own body best."

46. Indeed, we press the exclusive homily of Chrysostom, *hom. 49. operis imperf. in Matth.*: "In no way is it known to those who wish to know which is the true Christian Church except through the Scriptures alone."

47. The Word of God, which today does not exist except in the prophetic and apostolic Scriptures, is the seed, is the foundation, is the soul of the Church. If the Church strays from the path of God's Word, it strays into errors. And the further it drifts away from the purity of the Word, the more serious the errors.

48. From this, one can easily gather what our answer must be to the question of whether the Church can err.

49. For one must distinguish between the catholic Church and particular churches.

50. Then one must distinguish between errors which overturn the foundation and the stubble which is built upon the foundation.

51. Finally, one must distinguish between the Visible Church and the Invisible.

52. The Romanists, when they have argued long and loudly enough about the infallible judgment of the Church, in the end lead us back to the pope alone. That very infallibility, says Bellarmine (4. *de Pontif. c. 2.*), is not in the assembly of the advisers, or in the Council of Bishops, but in the pope alone...

53. The faithful people do not err if they follow their pastors. The pastors do not err if they follow their bishops. The bishops do not err, if they follow the pope. Therefore, the Church's immunity to error comes down to them from the pope alone.

54. What they attribute to the pope, we attribute to Christ, who teaches the Church in and through the Scriptures. The Church does not err, insofar and as long as it follows the voice of Christ and the direction of the Holy Spirit.

55. Finally, to that end God gathers the Church, that He may have, in this life and in the life to come, an assembly by which

He is rightly acknowledged, worshiped, and glorified.

56. The Church Militant on earth is the nursery of the Church Triumphant in heaven. May Christ, the Head of the Church, join us to the Church Triumphant. To Him be glory forever!

Chapter 20: The Ecclesiastical Ministry

1. There are three estates or orders in the Church, all of them established by God: the ecclesiastical, the political, and the domestic.

2. They are commonly called 'the three hierarchies.'

3. The ecclesiastical order is called in the Scriptures the 'ministry and the liturgy,' διακονία καὶ λειτουργία.

4. Therefore it is not any sort of despotic domination.

5. In this ecclesiastical ministry, one must consider both the legitimate call to it and the faithful administration of it.

6. The Church's call to the ministers is by all means necessary, and it must be a legitimate call.

7. For how will they preach unless they are sent? (Rom. 10:15).

8. The right to call ministers belongs to God. He, as the Lord of the harvest, sends out workers into His harvest (Mat. 9:38).

9. However, God calls the ministers of the Church both immediately and mediately.

10. The immediate call is characteristic of the prophets in the Old Testament and of the apostles in the New.

11. St. Paul describes it in this way in Gal. 1:1: It is done by God Himself, not by men nor through men.

12. This description is in no way contradicted by the fact that this call of God is sometimes declared externally by some prophet or apostle, or even by lot.

13. Certain extraordinary divine gifts and testimonies always attend an immediate call.

14. And yet we do not want those gifts and testimonies to be understood as miracles.

15. Indeed, John the Baptist performed no sign (John 10:41), and yet he was certainly called immediately.

16. But with regard to those testimonies of an immediate call, one should understand the peculiar demonstration of the Spirit and the remarkable efficacy of their ministry.

17. One is simply to have faith in the doctrine of those who have been called immediately by God, inasmuch as they are moved by the Spirit of God (2 Pet. 1:21).

18. This is why we are said to be built on the foundation of the prophets and apostles (Eph. 2:20).

19. For since they have been called in this way, they also have this privilege: that they are not bound to a certain church in a certain location, but have been given the authority to preach anywhere.

20. From this, it is clear that such a call is chiefly appropriate, either for establishing the Church, or for purging it from errors.

21. A mediate call is one which is made by God through suitable men according to the rule expressed in the Word of God.

22. Here one must note most carefully that the mediate call is no less divine than the other call that is immediate.

23. For it is God who appoints in the Church, not only prophets, apostles, and evangelists, but also pastors and teachers (1 Cor. 12:28, Eph. 4:11).

24. The ministers of the Church at Ephesus are said to have been appointed by the Holy Spirit, although Paul had commended the ministry to them by the laying on of hands (Acts 20:28).

25. Still today the Holy Spirit convicts the world through the ministry of those who are mediately called (John 16:8).

26. God carries out that mediate call by means of the ministry of the Church.

27. For to her, God has entrusted the deposit of His Word (Rom. 3:2). To her He has entrusted the Sacraments. To her, as to

his Bride, He has committed the keys of the kingdom of heaven (Mat. 18:17).

28. Therefore, the right to call ministers belongs to the whole Church, but in the definite manner and order expressed in the Scriptures.

29. How we are to understand this manner and order of calling is clear from the commandments and practice of the apostles.

30. The apostle says in 1 Cor. 16:3, "Whomever you approve by your letters, these I shall send." 1 Tim. 3:7, "It is necessary that the bishop have a good testimony." 1 Tim. 5:22, "Do not lay hands on anyone quickly," namely, before the testimony and consensus of the Church is added.

31. Join to this also the apostolic practice. Acts 6:3, in the election and ordination of deacons, the apostles speak thus: "Seek out brothers from among you, seven men adorned with suitable testimony, full of the Holy Spirit and wisdom, whom we may put in charge of this business." Acts 14:23, the elders are appointed by vote (elected by the raising of hands) in every Church.

32. From this proceed the verdicts of those ancient canons: No rule permits that they be considered among the bishops who are neither elected by the clergy, nor requested by the people, nor consecrated by the bishops of the same province, together with the judgment of the metropolitan bishop (*c. nulla. dist. 62. ex Leone Ep. Rom.*).

33. Likewise: Let them be requested by the people, elected by the clergy, ordained by the judgment of the bishops.

34. Likewise: Let those who will be priests be requested by the bishops. Let the endorsement of the clergy, the testimony of honorable men, and the consensus of the people be obtained.

35. Particularly noteworthy is the passage of Cyprian (*lib. 1. Epist. 4*). The people, above all, have the authority either to elect

worthy priests, or to reject the unworthy. We see that this very thing descends from divine authority, that the priest is elected in the presence of the people, before the eyes of all, and is shown to be worthy and fit by public judgment and testimony.

36. For this reason, since the right of calling ministers belongs to the whole Church, neither the presbytery alone, nor the magistrate alone, nor the remaining multitude should claim or usurp this right to themselves alone.

37. For that which affects all should be addressed by all.

38. But everything should be done in order, and confusions should be avoided (1 Cor. 14).

39. The public and solemn attestation of this call is the rite of ordination, by which, in the sight of God and in the presence of the whole Church, through the laying on of hands, the person who has been legitimately called is separated from the rest of the multitude for this office and commended to God with prayer, and public testimony is given to the call that was previously issued.

40. We deny that ordination is a Sacrament, if the word 'Sacrament' is understood properly and strictly.

41. For it lacks the external element expressly instituted by Christ Himself in the New Testament; it also lacks the promise concerning the application and sealing of grace which is characteristic of the Gospel.

42. Ordination is preceded by a careful examination by which one investigates the confession, the erudition, the gift for teaching, and the life of the one who is to be ordained.

43. The standard for this examination is set forth in 1 Tim. 3 and Tit. 1.

44. In these passages, such virtues are required of the one to whom the task of teaching in the Church is to be committed, as are either common to him together with other truly pious men, or as are proper and peculiar to him.

45. The common virtues are that he should be blameless, the husband of one wife, temperate, sober-minded, of good behavior, hospitable, not given to wine, not violent, not greedy for money, but gentle, not quarrelsome, not covetous, etc. (1 Tim. 3:2–4 ff., Titus 1:6–8).

46. The apostle mentions these common virtues because integrity of life is required of ministers, not only for the reasons which apply to other Christians, but also peculiarly for this reason: that their ministry may not be subject to false accusations, and thus an impediment, or certainly a hindrance, be brought upon the word as it bears fruit.

47. The apostle requires of the bishop that he be the husband of one wife in order to stop the mouths of the heretics who disparage marriage, thus demonstrating that marriage is not impure, but so honorable that even someone who wants to ascend the sacred throne of the episcopate can enter into it. (Chrysostom in *cap. 1. Epist. Tit.*).

48. Therefore, celibacy is not added to the Ecclesiastical Order by divine right.

49. For that 'self-control' which the apostle requires in the bishop is only to be understood of a vow of celibacy if it is first demonstrated that there is no self-control in the marriage of the godly (Ecclesiasticus 26:20, Gal. 5:22).

50. The apostle does not, with his pronouncement, keep away from the ministry those who have legitimately taken to themselves another wife after the death of their first wife.

51. But he does prohibit them to be chosen for the ministry who sin against the Sixth Commandment in any way, so that they are not the husbands of one wife.

52. For example, if they live in adultery, if they have several wives at the same time, if they take another wife after abandoning or divorcing their legitimate wife (except in the case of adultery), or

if they choose for themselves a woman who has been divorced by another.

53. But he also does not prescribe marriage as an absolute necessity for all the ministers of the Church; he leaves marriage open to them and subjects married ministers to the divinely ordained laws of marriage.

54. The special virtues which the apostle requires of the Church's ministers are these: they should be apt to teach (1 Tim. 3:2), equipped with the gift of teaching. Able also to encourage in the sound doctrine and to reprove those who contradict (Titus 1:9).

55. These things have been said concerning the legitimate call to the ministry. Now follows a discussion of the faithful administration of the same.

56. By faithful administration of the ministry, we understand all the duties of the ecclesiastical ministry, using the example of the apostle in 1 Cor. 4:1: "Let a man so esteem us as ministers of Christ and stewards of the mysteries of God." And verse 2, "But now this alone is required in a steward, that he be found faithful."

57. That faithfulness consists in this: that the affairs committed to the Church by God be administered as prescribed by God.

58. The affairs of the Church have in view either doctrine, or the Sacraments, or discipline.

59. Therefore the office of the ministers is restricted to the legitimate administration of doctrine, the Sacraments, and discipline.

60. The administration of doctrine consists both in the assertion of truth and in the refutation of error.

61. The standard both for teaching as well as reproving is the Word of God alone (2 Tim. 3:16).

62. The interpretation of the Holy Scripture pertains to teaching, and the application of Scripture pertains to the use of the Church.

63. The object and the manner must be kept in view in the administration of the Sacraments.

64. We understand the object to be that providential care by which the minister is supposed to consider beforehand to whom the Sacraments should be administered, or who should be prevented from receiving from them.

65. And this is the chief reason why private Confession and Absolution are retained in our churches, though other major reasons are not lacking.

66. The manner of administration means that, according to the command of Christ, they should be administered decently and in order.

67. Ecclesiastical discipline is carried out both in correcting those who have fallen and in exercising ecclesiastical judgments.

68. Those who have fallen must be corrected according to the steps prescribed by Christ (Mat. 18:15).

69. For admonition should come first, both private and public. If this admonition is despised by the manifest sinner, then let that severe administration of ecclesiastical judgment follow, which consists in excommunication.

70. Excommunication (the second part of the Keys) is either lesser or greater.

71. It is lesser when the sinner is temporarily forbidden from participating in the Supper.

72. It is greater when, after a legitimate examination, a willfully disobedient sinner is excluded from the fellowship of the Church and handed over to Satan.

73. The former is called ἀφορισμός, the latter ἀνάθεμα.

74. If only the chains of ecclesiastical discipline were more tightly bound in this worn-out old world than we commonly see being done!

75. The authority to excommunicate belongs to the whole Church and is carried out by the ministry on the Church's behalf.

76. Therefore, let the express or the tacit consensus of the Church be added. The apostle says in 1 Cor. 5:4, "While you are gathered together and in my Spirit, in the name of our Lord Jesus Christ, hand such a man over to Satan."

77. As for the legitimate call of ministers, so also for this administration of Church discipline, the Roman Pontiff is unjust.

78. For he removes from the magistrate and from the Christian people the right to elect ministers and claims it for the bishops alone, and most of all for himself.

79. He boasts that he is the Monarch, Head, and Bridegroom of the Church.

80. But from this very thing and from many other marks, we identify him as the Antichrist.

81. For the lessons of history and of experience testify that, whatever marks the Scripture attributes to the Antichrist, each and every one of them applies to the Roman Pontiff.

82. Likewise, the Roman Pope sins in many ways against the administration of ecclesiastical discipline.

83. For he claims for himself alone the supreme authority to excommunicate, absolve, administer, reserve cases, confer indulgences, benefits and similar things, propose, establish and enforce laws, control the ecclesiastical hierarchy, etc. (Franc. Vargas, *de jurisd. Episc.*).

84. He boasts that this authority rests in him as in a fountain and flows from him to the bishops as rivers.

85. He makes presbyters subject to bishops and grants them far less authority of jurisdiction.

86. We neither remove the order among the Church's ministers, nor do we approve the confusion of them. However, we

declare that the same authority of jurisdiction applies to all the Church's ministers.

87. Jerome shows in Tit. 1. that, at the time of the apostles, it was the same thing to be a bishop and an elder. And Michael Medina acknowledges (*lib. 1. de sacror. homin. origin. and cont. cap. 5.*) that Ambrose, Augustine, Sedulius, Primasius, Chrysostom, Theodoret, Oecumenius and Theophilact were all of the same opinion.

88. This, too, should be rejected in the practice of papal excommunication: that its thunder strikes against whole cities, whole provinces, whole kingdoms on account of only a few men, or even just one.

89. Nor does he practice excommunication on account of atheism or other shameful things, but, as the histories testify, it comes most often from personal hatred, levity, ambition, and a desire to dominate.

90. He also confuses this ecclesiastical discipline with civil penalties, as he strips excommunicated kings and emperors of kingdom and empire, frees their subjects from the homage and oaths due to them, and gives away their property to all as booty.

91. Finally, as to the purpose of papal excommunication, one should consult the histories. Especially notable are the writings of Rodericus Zamorensis (*in speculo vitae humanae lib. 2. cap. 3.*), Nicol. de Cleman. (*lib. de Ruin. et reparat. Eccles.*), whose testimony in this area is very accurate.

92. From these and similar abuses, there is no doubt that the highly beneficial aspect of ecclesiastical discipline has today all but collapsed. For other reasons for this, one should certainly consult Dr. Luther in his commentary on Joel 3 (*tom. 4. Jen. f. 801 ff.*). Read them and weigh them carefully.

93. O Christ, who sends out workers into Your harvest, the hour is coming for You to reap, for earth's harvest is parched and its grapes are ripe (Rev. 14:15, 18). Let him who loves You say, 'Come!' Amen.

Chapter 21: The Political Order

1. On account of the intercession and merit of the Son, both the eternal goods and those of this life—both of which the human race destroyed by its apostasy—have been restored by God.

2. Through the ministry of the Word, God gathers to Himself the Church, by which He is rightly acknowledged and worshiped, in whose true members He restores His image and begins eternal life.

3. But since the gathering of this Church and the restoration of the divine image occurs in this life, God has instituted the political order, that it may be a kind of hedge for the Church.

4. For to this end God has granted the government to kings and to all those who hold lofty positions of authority, that we may lead a quiet and peaceable life under them, in all godliness and discipline (1 Tim. 2:2).

5. The Church is gathered from the human race. After the fall, the human race has been miserably corrupted and cannot exist stably without political government. By all means, therefore, it was necessary for the sake of the Church that the State be instituted.

6. There are two parts of the political order: the magistrate and the subjects.

7. The magistrate rules; the subjects are ruled.

8. The magistrate is either higher or lower. 1 Pet. 2:13–14: "Be subject to every human institution, whether to the king as supreme, or to rulers, as those sent by him."

9. The higher magistrate enjoys full control; the lower rules over others in such a way that it is still subject to the higher.

10. Each is divinely ordained, for there is no authority except from God (Rom. 13:1).

11. Therefore, it is certainly not forbidden for the Christian to hold the office of magistrate.

12. For the Gospel does not abolish the State, nor do divine institutions mutually destroy one another.

13. God calls a person to the magistrate either mediately or immediately.

14. We have examples of an immediate call in Moses, David, etc. For with His own voice God called them, immediately and extraordinarily, to rule over His people.

15. The mediate call takes place chiefly in two manners, either by hereditary succession, or by an election on the part of men. The other forms of the mediate call can be traced back to one of these two manners.

16. Those who are called mediately to the magistrate are to be considered as divinely established and appointed, no less than those who are called immediately by the divine voice.

17. For when Peter calls them a 'human institution' (1 Pet. 2:13), he says it, not because it is merely a human institution, but because it is performed by men; because the magistrate is constituted from among men; and because its constitution exists for the benefit of human society.

18. The office of magistrate is viewed either in peace or in war.

19. In a time of peace, he should administer justice and judgment.

20. By justice is understood the external obedience which is owed to both tables of the Decalogue.

21. For the magistrate is to be the guardian of both tables with regard to external discipline.

22. The magistrate both can and should: prevent false and blasphemous dogmas from being proliferated; restrain the par-

ticularly seditious deceivers of souls; forbid the profaning of the Sabbath.

23. At the same time, however, he should not pretend to rule over the consciences of men, of which God Himself is King.

24. Therefore, the magistrate should neither compel his subjects toward false religion, nor should they submit to the demands of the magistrate who thus compels them.

25. To be sure, the magistrate neither can nor should coerce anyone even toward the true religion.

26. He cannot do this, because by simply extorting an external profession, he creates hypocrites. He should not do it, because religion should be undertaken willingly, not by compulsion or force.

27. Tertullian puts it beautifully, *ad Scap. Religionis*, No one should be compelled to religion.

28. That famous saying of the most laudable Emperor Maximilian II concurs with this: There is nothing more intolerable than the desire to rule as lord over men's consciences.

29. To the administration of justice belongs the authority to enact civil laws, which are to serve as boundaries of the law of nature.

30. For the political affairs of Christians are not simply bound to the forensic laws of Moses.

31. To this administration of justice belong contracts, which should be tempered with love and equity. Accordingly, it can easily be determined what one should conclude in the question of usury.

32. The Scripture simply prohibits usury. But which contracts are usurious must be discerned from the purpose of the law, which is love, from the description of the prohibition, and from the uncorrupted judgment of the wise.

33. By judgment we understand the defense of the good and the punishment of the wicked (Rom. 13:4).

34. To this end, forensic courts have been introduced, in which a discovery is made of the cases, both civil and criminal.

35. Therefore, it is not forbidden to the Christian to litigate in court, as long as it is done legitimately.

36. The punishment which the magistrate inflicts on those who transgress the laws and disturb human society should correspond to the guilt.

37. For the magistrate is not free to remit altogether the penalties imposed on lawbreakers, especially in an erratic manner.

38. But clemency should sometimes be shown, with a consideration for the wrongdoer and the crime itself.

39. As the highest offense often diminishes the highest law, so on the other hand an untimely indulgence diminishes the authority of the law and of the magistrate.

40. Some ask in this regard whether heresy, theft, and adultery should be capital offenses.

41. We deny that capital punishment should be inflicted upon a person who personally holds to a heretical opinion, or even upon him who spreads it without sedition.

42. But we leave to the magistrate the other methods of coercing those who spread heresies.

43. We call it harsh to say that the punishment for simple theft, especially minor theft, should always be capital.

44. At the same time, we do not disapprove severe laws against thieves, intruders, and those who commit theft repeatedly.

45. The divine Law itself prescribes the penalty of the sword to adultery.

46. In a time of war, the magistrate likewise must remember his office, so that he wages war legitimately.

47. For it is not forbidden either to the magistrate to declare war, or to the subjects to wage it, as long as it is done legitimately.

48. The conditions of legitimate war are that it must be

waged by the authority of the superiors, that the cause must be just, and that the intention must be good (Thomas, 2. 2. *q. 40.*).

49. If it is waged without the legitimate authority of the one who declares war, it is not war, but highway robbery.

50. There are three just causes of war: just defense, just punishment, or legitimate recovery.

51. The intention of an agreeable end must likewise be present. The desire should be for peace; war should be waged of necessity. Therefore, let war be waged that peace may be obtained (Augustine, *Epist.* 205.).

52. We include in a right intention also the legitimate manner of waging war.

53. Aurelianus puts it beautifully to the military tribunes: "If you want to be a tribune, if you want to live, restrain the hands of the soldiers. Let no one steal another's hen, let no one seize an egg, let no one snatch a grape, let no one pilfer from a grain field, let no one make off with oil, salt, or wood, but let him be content with his provisions. Let him live on the booty of the enemy, not the tears of the provincials."

54. Nor can it be hoped that those soldiers will handle their own affairs happily if they carry home with them curses and tears in their departure (Gregory, *lib. 6. Hist. c. 12.*).

55. Let them try their strength against an enemy, against whom we declare that military strategies are also permissible.

56. But the magistrate should attempt all things first, before taking up arms, nor should he resort to war unless extreme necessity of the republic demands it, just as doctors resort to cauterizations and incisions.

57. Just as when we, by our own decision, put money on a roll of the dice and it immediately takes on a strange legal status, uncertain to whom it will go, so the magistrate and the entire government, by the undertaking of war, is thrust into the fate of the outcome. (Luis Vives in a letter to Henry VIII, King of England.)

58. The second part of the political order is made up of the subjects, who are contrasted relatively with the magistrate.

59. Moreover, they are either merely subjects, or they are subjects who have been given some authority.

60. Subjects owe the magistrate honor, fear, loyalty, obedience, tribute, and prayer.

61. This honor must be in the heart, in the mouth, and in the external deed.

62. Let us view the magistrate as an institution of God. Let us neither detract from it with a cursing mouth, nor withdraw from it our external reverence.

63. There are certain limits to this obedience. For those who have been granted some authority are able to take the reins, as it were, of that growing power.

64. When are those who are merely subjects not held to obey the magistrate in all things? When something is commanded that goes against godliness or honor.

65. The power of fearful kings over their own flocks is the power of God over the kings themselves.[34]

66. Therefore, in this area, by fearing the authority (of God as the supreme Monarch), you hold in contempt the authority (the magistrate who commands unjust things).

67. If something is commanded that is heavy and difficult, it must be carried out. If something is commanded that is impious and wicked, then obedience must be denied.

68. Tributes are owed to the magistrate because of his work, because of his governance, and because of the defense he provides.

69. But due moderation should be observed here, which should be considered both from the ability of the subjects and from the necessity of the republic.

---

34   cf. Horace, *Odes, Book III:I*

70. One asks here whether the passage from 1 Sam. 8 deals with the right or with the custom? The matter can be decided with a distinction between the necessity of government and the desire of the governor.

71. The apostle expressly teaches in 1 Tim. 2:2 that prayers should be made for the magistrate.

72. Bugenhagen has put it well: "If we were as quick to pour out prayers for the magistrate as we are to disparage them, then our affairs would certainly be in a better state."

73. "Woe to the principality that buries its lords, say the teachers of the Hebrews!," as R. Salom. Jario reports in *Comment. Hos. 1*.

74. Indeed, Antigonus is often dug up by his subjects after his death.

75. Let things be said concerning the political order. The practice of the remaining things pertains to the political doctrine.

76. May God, who establishes kingdoms, grant to our magistrate perennial peace of rule, eternal salvation of body and soul. Amen.

Chapter 22: Marriage

1. Marriage is an estate instituted by God as man still persists in concreated integrity.

2. Therefore, let marriage be honorable among all and the bed undefiled (Heb. 13:4).

3. Nevertheless, it is not properly and accurately—that is, according to the definition that applies to Baptism and the Holy Supper—a Sacrament.

4. For it lacks the external and visible, divinely instituted element, and the promise of the characteristic grace of the Gospel.

5. Nevertheless, according to the generally and broadly understood term, it can be called a Sacrament, that is, a sign of a sacred thing (Eph. 5:32).

6. The proper *sedes doctrinae* concerning marriage is Gen. 2:18ff.

7. Christ calls us back to this in Mat. 19:5 and demonstrates that an analysis of marital questions must be taken up from this passage.

8. There it is taught that marriage is the legitimate and indissoluble union of two people only; namely, of one man and one woman.

9. Therefore, marriage is opposed to bigamy and polygamy.

10. Bigamy is not when a person whose first wife has died takes a second wife, but when a person has two wives at the same time (Chrysostom in *1 Tim.* 3.).

11. For neither a second marriage, nor a third, nor further marriages are forbidden by the Holy Scriptures, as long as they are established in the Lord.

12. For the reason for marrying does not die when the first spouse dies, but the same reason lives on all the more.

13. God tolerated the polygamy of the fathers in the Old Testament, but He certainly didn't command it.

14. Moreover, He tolerated it because they were not polygamous for the sake of unbridled lust, but out of zeal for propagating the Church and a zeal to promote the promise about the blessed Seed.

15. And thus God used their evil for good.

16. In order for the uniting of spouses to be legitimate, the consensus of both parties is required.

17. There must be no violence; there must be no error, especially such as affects the essential points of marriage.

18. But that consensus should be lawful, honorable, just, free, full, and sincere.

19. At the same time, not every error permits the pledge of matrimony previously given to be rescinded.

20. Nor should the betrothal be rescinded because of any and every defect in the marriage agreement.

21. Furthermore, the consent of those who contract marriage without parental consent is null and void.

22. Therefore, we say that parental consent is required, not only for the sake of the honor of those contracting marriage, but also by the law of necessity—

23. Having followed the authority of divine Law, natural law, and civil law—

24. Which even some of the canons of papal law, especially the older ones, approve.

25. If the parents are little mindful of their duty, or if they wish to abuse their parental authority, then let the magistrate fill the role of the parents.

26. For a legitimate union, it is also required that the degrees of consanguinity not be violated.

27. Moreover, it is taught in Lev. 18 and 20 which persons are allowed to be united by the bonds of matrimony, by the express limitation of degrees both of consanguinity and of relationship.

28. We say that those texts should be understood not only about the persons, but also about the degrees.

29. And we expressly affirm that those ordinances belong to the law of nature.

30. Therefore, there is no room for dispensation in them.

31. Therefore, to these divine Laws, for good and useful purpose of greater reverence, prohibitions have been added by godly magistrates up to the third degree of unequal line.

32. We declare that these prohibitions are likewise to be observed, although we permit them to be relaxed for probable cause.

33. Nevertheless, one must seriously see to it that such dispensation does not turn into dissipation.

34. In figuring the degrees, we follow the disposition of the canons.

35. Not because we acknowledge ourselves to be bound by the laws of the papal court, but because in this area they are sound and equitable.

36. On the straight line, it teaches this rule: As many as are the persons, so many are the levels, once removed.

37. In the collateral equal line, this rule is taught: By as many levels as one person is removed from his stock, by so many levels is he also removed from the other person.

38. In the collateral, unequal line, by as many levels as a person is further removed from his stock, by so many levels is he also removed from the other.

39. One must also abstain from certain marriages out of respect for affinity.

40. But that affinity which impedes matrimony does not go far.

41. For between the relatives of the husband and the relatives of the wife there is no such affinity that impedes matrimony.

42. But between the wife and the relatives of the husband and between the husband and the relatives of the wife there is an affinity that impedes matrimony.

43. Therefore, according to the constitutions of all laws, on the straight line the prohibition extends infinitely.

44. On the collateral line, the prohibition is extended by provincial laws up to the third degree of unequal line (inclusively).

45. And this has in view not only blood relation, but also affinity.

46. But canon law admonishes most rightly: In the union of matrimony, one must look not only at what is permissible, but also what is honorable.

47. The principal purpose of marriage is the propagation of the human race, and consequently also of the Church.

48. The lesser purposes are to have a faithful helper, and to have a type of Christ and the Church.

49. The accidental purpose is the avoidance of fornication.

50. For that which was instituted as a duty before the fall, has now, after the fall, become also a remedy.

51. It is not without reason that betrothal should come first, before the marriage is finalized.

52. Betrothal is the promise of a future marriage.

53. A betrothal can be rescinded for certain reasons, the adjudication of which belongs to men in the consistories who are pious, learned, and wise.

54. In general, we say that the repudiation of a prospective spouse can be made for more reasons than the divorce of a spouse.

55. For many things impede the contraction of marriage which do not dissolve a marriage already contracted.

56. Matrimony is dissolved by death and by adultery.

57. By adultery, the very bond of marriage is dissolved, so that it is permissible for the innocent party to take vows a second time.

58. Jerome thinks that an adulteress cannot be retained. Augustine thinks that an adulteress cannot be dismissed. We march along the middle road.

59. If a malicious deserter departs, the magistrate rightly advises the innocent party.

60. At the same time, however, the exclusive declaration of Christ does not permit a cause of divorce other than adultery.

61. That which is stated as an exception is not extended to other cases (Bald. *l. 28. C. de adult.*).

62. The inability of the body for the use of marriage does not cause a divorce; it proves that no marriage has ever occurred.

63. It serves for proof that an inability that arises after the marriage does not admit divorce.

64. Let the same judgment be made concerning an error in essential things.

65. Violence is likened to desertion.

66. We do not concede that a marriage is to be dissolved on account of heresy.

67. Virginity is subordinate to marriage, since, in both estates, chastity is pleasing to God.

68. The apostle prefers virginity to marriage—that is, in suitable persons who have been equipped with the gift of self-restraint, and, to a degree, on account of the troubles of marriage and the circumstances of the times.

69. The yoke of virginity should be imposed on no one unwillingly, since not all are capable of it.

70. Therefore, marriage is free to all; for those who burn, it is also necessary.

71. If a willing spirit makes you a virgin, you are truly a virgin. Neither vow nor coercion will be necessary.

72. If you are a virgin by coercion, you are not a virgin before God, nor will you be delivered by a vow.

73. The virginity of body without the virginity of the mind is hypocritical.

74. Virginity is not to be pitted against a pious and chaste marriage, but should be placed far behind it.

75. It is useless to keep the body unstained if the mind burns inwardly with burning flames of desire.

76. What good is flesh that is whole if the mind is corrupt?

77. But how many of those who vow virginity actually keep their body unstained in every way?

78. There are far fewer who have a mind that is free from burning lust.

79. The great apostle Paul never meant to create a law in this area or put a noose on anyone.

80. Therefore, if only those who are unable to remain abstinent would shudder at the mention of celibacy, for it is a costly tower and a grand word which not all are able to grasp! (Bernard, *serm. ad Cleric.*).

81. I have never known a woman, but I am not a virgin. (Cited from Basil by Cassianus, *lib. 6. de Spir. fornic.*).

82. A good man uses marriage well. An evil man uses neither marriage nor virginity rightly.

83. May Christ, the Bridegroom of the Church, accompany pious spouses, and may He one day transfer us all to the heavenly wedding banquet!

Chapter 23: The Four Final Things that Await Man

1. We have seen the situation of the Church Militant on earth. It remains for us to lift up our minds to a consideration of the Church Triumphant in heaven.

2. The transfer of the godly from the Church Militant to the Church Triumphant takes place through death, which Gregory of Nyssa very neatly compares to a midwife who brings us forth to the life that is truly so called.

3. Judgment follows death, of which the forerunner is the universal resurrection of all men. It is appointed for men to die once, and after that, the judgment (Heb. 9:27).

4. Those who have done good will go forth into the resurrection of life; but those who have done evil into the resurrection of judgment (John 5:29).

5. Therefore, there are four final things that await man. Let us never fail to remember and consider them carefully: Death, Resurrection, Judgment, and the Eternal Abode or Dwelling—of the godly in heaven, of the damned in hell.

6. With the word 'death' here, we understand, not those perpetual miseries of this mortal life (1 Cor. 15:31); nor that death of the soul in trespasses (Eph. 2:5); nor that blessed death by which we are dead to sin—that is, in which we live to God as those who have been set free from sin's dominion and condemnation (Rom. 6:2); nor that eternal or second death of the damned (Rev. 2:11).

7. Rather, we understand the death of the body, which is the separation of the soul from the body, the deprivation of biological life, and the passing away of the microcosm.

8. "He who dies to vices before he dies, does not die (with the body) with eternal death when he dies (with the death of the body)" (*Sphinx Phil. c. 36.*).

9. Death entered into the world through the gate of sin, and thus it passed over into all men (Rom. 5:12).

10. This death is not the annihilation of the soul, but the egress of the soul from the home of the body. The soul cannot be killed (Mat. 10:28).

11. Scripture mentions only two receptacles for the souls that have been separated from their bodies through death: one for the godly, the other for the wicked.

12. Therefore, farewell to purgatory; farewell to soul-sleep[35]; farewell to the Pythagoric transmigration of the soul[36]; farewell to the apparition of souls.

13. Nor is there any middle place where he who was not established in the kingdom is not in torment; so that he who was not with Christ may be somewhere else than with the devil (Augustine, *de pecc. mor. et remiss. c. 2.*).

14. The passing away of the macrocosm will precede the universal resurrection and will be followed by universal judgment.

15. Several of the fathers think that the world will pass away with a change of its qualities, but not with a substantial abolition of them.

16. Scripture uses very emphatic words: Heaven and earth will perish, will pass away, will disappear, will flee in such a way that a place for them cannot be found, etc.

17. The key to our graves and the deposit of our resurrection is the resurrection of Christ our Head.

18. Manifest and oft-repeated utterances of the Holy Spirit confirm the resurrection of our bodies.

---

35 *psychopannychia*
36 *metempsychosis*

19. The preludes of this resurrection are the particular examples of people who were resurrected in the Old and New Testaments, whom Tertullian calls, 'candidates of immortality.'

20. Man was once created, in both body and soul, for immortality. Our body is an instrument for the good or evil works of the soul. The body of the godly is the temple of the Holy Spirit. Our bodies, too, are nourished with the vivified body and blood of Christ. How, then, should they remain forever in the grave?

21. The Author of the resurrection is God. The Perfecter is Christ, in and with the assumed human nature.

22. Not only will all flesh arise, but even that same flesh which has died.

23. Analogous to the resurrection of the dead is the instantaneous change of those whom the Last Day will encounter still alive.

24. Christ will not only do the raising, but also the judging, for the Father has handed all judgment over to Him (John 5:27).

25. Christ will appear for judgment in that nature which He united to Himself through the incarnation. That very nature will be the Judge which stood before the judgment. That very nature which was once judged will judge.

26. The truth and righteousness of God require this universal judgment.

27. The experience of the things that happen at that time will teach the exact form, mode, and process of the judgment better than the understanding of men is currently able perfectly to grasp.

28. Let us sigh to be freed on that day from a harsh word. Let us hear the voice of Him who invites us, that one day we may hear the voice of Him who consoles us.

29. A broad sentence will immediately be given for execution. Those who have been placed on the right hand of the Judge will go to eternal life; those on His left will be cast out into eternal fire (Mat. 25:26).

30. The happiness of eternal life includes the removal of evil and the addition of good. There will be an absence of all that is evil and the full enjoyment of all that is good.

31. We will be freed from sin; we will be freed from all the penalties of sin.

32. Our body will be conformed to the body of Christ (Phi. 3:21), save for a difference in glory.

33. We will see God without end, we will love without contempt, we will praise without growing weary (Augustine, 22. *de Civitat. Dei ca.* 30.).

34. Sight will replace faith; perfect enjoyment will replace hope. There will be a most perfect consummation of love.

35. God will be the fullness of light to the intellect, the multitude of peace to the will, the continuation of eternity for our memory (Bernard, *serm. 11. super Cant. Col.* 519.).

36. The saints will rejoice on account of the pleasantness of the place which they will possess; on account of the delightful fellowship in which they will reign; on account of the glorification of the body which they will enjoy; on account of the world which they have scorned; on account of the hell which they have avoided (Bonvent. in *Dioet. c.* 50.).

37. Therefore, let us sigh for that life whose King is the Trinity, whose law is love, whose limit is eternity.

38. Our being will be without death; our knowing will be without error; our love will be without offense (*Sph. Phil,. pag.* 5.).

39. We will see God with His own face; we will hear Him with His own voice.

40. Of all the elect there will be the highest knowledge, perfect righteousness, eternal happiness, everlasting praise.

41. There will be one common salvation, but a disparate glory.

42. It has not entered into the heart of man what glory God has prepared for His elect (1 Cor. 2:9). How much less shall we

understand with words the condition of that glory?

43. With the eternal life of the blessed is contrasted the eternal death of the damned, the second death spoken of in Revelation.

44. The life of the damned will be deadly, and death will be undying. If it is life, why does it kill? If it is death, how does it last forever?

45. The damned will live in such a way that they are ever dying. They will die in such a way that they are ever alive (Bernard, in *med. devot. cap. 3. col. 193.*).

46. They will be tortured in the flesh through fire, in the soul through the worm of conscience (Bernard, in *med. devot. cap. 3. col. 193.*).

47. It is an eternity of punishments—an eternity which increases the torment of the damned beyond all measure.

48. Indeed, it is reported, beyond all bounds of despair, that they must be tormented without end (Isidor. *Clar. Orat. 12.*).

49. The punishment of the damned is heavy on account of the severity of the torment, heavier on account of the diversity of sufferings, heaviest on account of the eternity of the sufferings (Dionysius in *18. Apocal. f. 301.*).

50. The door will be closed to them (Mat. 25:10): the door of indulgence, the door of mercy, the door of hope, the door of consolation, the door of good activity.

51. To have been alienated from the sight of God will surpass all the punishments of Gehenna.

52. Those who are oppressed by the weight of such punishments will wish they could cease to exist, but in vain; they will desire death, but death will flee from them (Rev. 9:6).

53. They will growl, they will rage, they will gnash their teeth at their heart's inability to endure the anguish. There will be wailing from pain and gnashing of teeth from rage (Bernard, *serm. 8. in Psal. 91.*).

54. There are some who receive a foretaste of all these things in this life.

55. The fellowship of the devils and the nature of the place increase the punishments of the damned in no small way.

56. The punishments of the damned will be not only eternal, but without interruption (Rev. 14:11).

57. Whereas in heaven one person will be more glorious than another, so in hell one person will be more miserable than another (Augustine, in *Enchirid. cap. 3.*).

58. One asks out of curiosity where hell is. One would do better to consider how we might escape its punishments.

59. If only hell were mentioned among us at all times, when we eat lunch or supper, when we rise from our beds or when we retire for the evening!

60. For to mention hell does not cause a person to fall into it (Chrysostom, *hom. 44. in Matth.*).

61. But if you are silent about hell, you haven't extinguished its flames, have you? Nor have you fanned its flames by speaking about it. Whether you speak of it or not, its flames will still burn (Chrysostom, *homil. 2. in 2. Thessal.*).

62. May He who died for us free us from eternal death. May He who is the Leader of life—blessed forever!—lead us to eternal life.

THE END

www.ingramcontent.com/pod-product-compliance
Lightning Source LLC
Chambersburg PA
CBHW061603110426
42742CB00039B/2744